Restaurant
Graphics & Interiors

EAT AND
STAY

Wang Shaoqiang
(ed.)

Branding et intérieurs
de restaurants

Grafismo e interiorismo
de restaurantes

promopress

EAT and STAY

Restaurant Graphics & Interiors
Branding et intérieurs de restaurants
Grafismo e interiorismo de restaurantes

Editor: Wang Shaoqiang
English preface revised by: Tom Corkett
Translators of the preface:
Aurélie Chamerois, French translation
Jesús de Cos Pinto, Spanish translation

Copyright © 2016 by Sandu Publishing Co., Ltd.
Copyright © 2016 English language edition by
Promopress for sale in Europe and America.
PROMOPRESS is a brand of:
Promotora de Prensa Internacional S.A.
C/ Ausiàs March, 124
08013 Barcelona, Spain
Phone: 0034 93 245 14 64
Fax: 0034 93 265 48 83
info@promopress.es
www.promopresseditions.com
Facebook: Promopress Editions
Twitter: Promopress Editions @PromopressEd
Sponsored by Design 360°
– Concept and Design Magazine
Edited and produced by
Sandu Publishing Co., Ltd.
Book design, concepts & art direction by
Sandu Publishing Co., Ltd.
info@sandupublishing.com

Cover design:
spread: David Lorente

ISBN 978-84-16504-09-1

Printed in China

CONTENTS

006 – 008   Preface by Blacksheep

010 – 013   Mikôto Japanese Cuisine

014 – 017   Puebla 109

018 – 019   Franco

020 – 021   Nozomi Sushi Bar

022 – 023   The Newmans' Eat Dine & Whisky

024 – 027   The Pelican Seafood Bar & Grill

028 – 031   Céltorony

032 – 035   enfant terrible, Bar & Café

036 – 039   Mantra Raw Vegan

040 – 043   Grüner Michel Vegetarian Restaurant

044 – 045   Ask for Luigi

046 – 047   Casa Virginia

048 – 051   El Imparcial

052 – 055   Ninigi

056 – 057   Lanes of London, Marriott London

058 – 061   Set Cafè

062 – 065   Restaurant Vora Estany

066 – 067   BA 53

068 – 071   Simple

072 – 073   The Gorgeous Kitchen

074 – 075   Park Restaurant + Distillery

076 – 079   Bord 13

080 – 081   Época

082 – 083   Gillray's Steakhouse & Bar

084 – 087   Magno Brasserie

088 – 089   O'Petit en'K

090 – 093   Home Bakery

094 – 097   BARBA Restaurant

098 – 101   Krystian's Kitchen

102 – 103   Artigiano

104 – 105   Sean's Kitchen Adelaide

106 – 107   Kaldi Azul

108 – 111   Scheu's Essen & Trinken

112 – 115   Bambudda

116 – 117   Malahat - Speakeasy & Mixology

118 – 119   MexOut

120 – 121   Allegrezza

122 – 123   Local Mbassy

124 – 127   Raqpart

128 – 131   Hay Market

132 – 133   Blacktail Florist

134 – 135   Burger Circus

136 – 137   Revolver

138 – 139   Bowery Lane

140 – 143   4ECK Restaurant and Bar

144 – 147	Aguafuerte
148 – 151	Russ & Daughters Cafe
152 – 155	Mamva
156 – 157	Sushi & Co
158 – 159	MET
160 – 161	Violet Oon Singapore
162 – 163	Bovino Steakhouse
164 – 165	Le Saint Cochon
166 – 167	Misegreta
168 – 169	SO 9
170 – 171	THE GRAIN STORE
172 – 173	Mosquito
174 – 175	Madam Sixty Ate
176 – 177	EVVA
178 – 179	Sal Curioso
180 – 181	Tamarindo
182 – 183	Flamingo Restaurant & Bistro
184 – 185	El Passatge
186 – 187	Pidgin
188 – 189	Costa Nueva
190 – 193	Karhu
194 – 197	DOB3
198 – 199	Alberto Senties
200 – 201	The Clifford Pier
202 – 203	Lonfood
204 – 205	La Florentina
206 – 207	12/10
208 – 209	RIB'Z grill&booze
210 – 213	Ananda Vegan Restaurant
214 – 215	Oldhand Coffee
216 – 217	22 Ships
218 – 219	OCF
220 – 221	Sandinha
222 – 225	Botanero Moritas
226 – 227	Tartares & Co
228 – 231	Table Manners
233 – 239	Index
240	Acknowledgements

PREFACE

Eating and drinking have always been intrinsic to our lives, but in recent years the culture surrounding them has exploded. The food and drink industry has rushed to fill the void left in free time by retail's progressive migration to the online world, and going out for a meal has become many people's chosen leisure activity. Never before have we cared more about what we are eating and drinking or where we are seen doing it. Whole festivals are dedicated to the art of brewing the perfect coffee. You can grab a meal from a Michelin-starred chef before catching a flight. Blink and you'll miss the latest street-food concept. The sheer number of options that have sprung up to cater to this hungry market is staggering.

This unprecedented competitiveness within the market has been accompanied by a shift in perceptions of what makes a great night out. A meal and drinks once meant fine dining and all the luxurious trappings that went with it. Now the value and social currency are in the experience.

In striving to offer these ever more surprising experiences, the food and beverage world continues to merge and collaborate with the art, design, technology and entertainment industries, and the boundaries between them are becoming increasingly blurred. Companies that have never traditionally been associated with food and beverages are becoming involved in the sector in unexpected ways.

Within this explosion of outlets and abundance of experiences, guests have become more discerning. They are well travelled and well fed. They know what good kimchi is and how it is served. They've tasted burritos from a roadside stand in Mexico or visited an authentic Italian gelateria. They expect and know a standard of quality, and they can smell and taste inauthenticity a mile off.

Any brand that wants to find its place within this cluttered and competitive market needs to work harder than ever. As designers, we are in the business of improving people's lives by delivering a memorable experience. Creating that experience means thinking about every touch point.

Good brands will have clear values, behaviours and stories. Good branding and interior design translate these elements by engineering the ambience of a space and ensuring clarity and consistency throughout the guest's experience. Achieving these aims requires going beyond the physical space. Tableware, uniforms, service style and even the way in which staff members communicate: all of these must relate to what you are putting on the plate.

But the value of good design doesn't end with providing a memorable guest experience. Whether it takes the form of getting more bums on seats through intelligent layouts or improving staff retention by creating an environment that people are proud to work in, good design can be a powerful business tool. In such a competitive marketplace, it can give modern restaurants the edge.

Our studio always approaches a project by seeking out the brand's spirit and what the guest experience needs to be. When the Marriott approached Blacksheep to work on Gillray's Steakhouse & Bar at the Marriott County Hall, the spirit was easy to identify. Named after the famed eighteenth-century caricaturist James Gillray and boasting a menu that showcases the best of English produce, from Aberdeen Angus steak to Dover sole, Gillray's needed to offer a quintessentially eccentric English experience. Every creative decision took its lead from this. From the nine-metre-long Chesterfield sofa to the Sheffield silverware and English-oak table tops through to a peppering of James Gillray's satirical illustrations throughout the menus and branding, there is a holistic nature to the design solution. The drinks menu completes the experience by offering guests a selection of thirty-nine of the best English gins and cocktails with names such as Death on the Thames and Gin Hound.

Now more than ever, a good product constitutes just one aspect in an experience-led food and drink industry. In order to inspire loyalty and preference, a visual identity that perfectly reflects a bar's or restaurant's culinary philosophy will ensure that the establishment stands out. *Eat & Stay* showcases just such success stories. The following pages profile remarkable branding and interior solutions from across the world. They have given restaurants the unique qualities needed in today's food-culture explosion.

by Blacksheep

A London-based independent, international, and award winning design agency specialized in food & beverage industry.

PRÉFACE

Manger et boire ont toujours fait partie de nos vies, mais ces dernières années la culture les entourant a explosé. L'industrie agro-alimentaire s'est dépêchée de remplir le vide laissé par la progressive migration du commerce de distribution vers le monde en ligne, et sortir pour prendre un repas est devenu pour beaucoup une activité de loisirs. Jamais auparavant nous ne nous étions autant préocupé de ce que nous mangions et buvions, et d'où nous allions le faire. Des festivals entiers sont dédiés à l'art de réaliser le parfait café. Vous pouvez d'attraper un repas signé d'un chef étoilé au Michelin avant d'attraper votre vol. En un clin d'oeil, vous pourriez manquer les derniers concepts de street-food (ou *manger dans la rue*). L'incroyable nombre d'options qui ont fleuri sur ce marché affamé est en train d'exploser.

La concurrence sans précédent sur ce marché a été accompagnée par un changement de perception sur ce qui rend une soirée unique. Un repas rimait avant avec de fins mets et toute la décoration luxueuse qui allait avec. Aujourd'hui la valeur se trouve dans l'expérience.

Dans sa lutte pour offrir des expériences toujours plus surprenants, le monde du boire et du manger continuer à se fondre et à collaborer avec celui de l'art, de design, de la technologie et des industries du divertissement. Et les frontières deviennent de plus en plus floues. Les entreprises traditionnellement associés à l'alimentaire deviennent de plus en plus impliquées dans des secteurs inattendus.

Avec l'explosion des lieux et l'abondance des expériences, les clients sont devenus plus perspicaces. Ils voyagent beaucoup, ils mangent de tout. Ils savent ce qu'est un bon kichmi et comment il doit être servi. Ils ont testé les burritos dans un stand au bord de la route au Mexique et ont visité une authentique fabrique de glaces italiennes. Ils attendent et connaissent les standards de qualité, et ils peuvent sentir l'inauthenticité à deux kilomètres.

Toute marque qui veut trouver sa place dans ce marché concurrentiel doit travailler encore plus dur qu'avant. En tant que designers, nous sommes dans le business visant à améliorer la vie des gens en leur offrant une expérience inoubliable. Créer cette expérience signifie penser à tous ses aspects.

Les bonnes marques vont avoir des valeurs, des histoires et des comportements clairs. Une bonne gestion de la marque et du design d'intérieur vont traduire ces éléments dans la création de l'ambiance d'un espace, s'assurant de sa clarté et de sa consistance à travers l'expérience client. Accomplir ces objectifs requière d'aller plus loin que l'espace physique. Vaisselle, uniformes, style du service et même la manière dont le personnel communique : tout cela doit raconter ce que vous mettez dans l'assiette.

Mais la valeur d'un bon design ne s'arrête pas à livrer une expérience client inoubliable. Que cela passe par mettre plus de coussins dans les sièges ou garder plus longtemps les employés en créant un environnement où les gens sont fiers de travailler, un bon design peut être un puissant outil. Dans un marché aussi compétitif, cela peut faire la différence.

Notre studio débute toujours son approche d'un projet en recherchant l'esprit de la marque et ce que l'expérience client devrait être. Quand Marriot a approché Blacksheep pour travailler sur le Gillray's Steakhouse & Bar au Marriott County Hall, l'esprit était facile à identifier. Tirant son nom du célèbre caricaturiste du 18e siècle James Gillray et offrant un menu avec le meilleur des produits anglais, du steak Aberdeen Angus à la sole de Douvres, Gillray's avait besoin d'offir une expérience excentrique de quintessence anglaise. Chaque décision créative a pris naissance de là. Depuis le sofa Chesterfield de neuf mètres de long au service Sheffield ou aux tables en chêne anglais jusqu'aux illustrations satiriques de James Gillray sur les menus, il y a une cohérence naturelle dans les solutions de design apportées. Les cartes des boissons complètent l'expérience en offrant une sélection de 39 des meilleurs gins et cocktails anglais, avec des noms tels que Mort sur la Tamise ou Le Chien de Chasse du Gin.

Maintenant plus que jamais, un bon produit n'est pas juste un aspect de l'expérience culinaire. Afin d'inspirer confiance et fidélité, une identité visuelle qui reflète parfaiement la philosophie culinaire du bar ou du restaurant assurera longévité à l'établissement. *Eat & Stay* fait état de plusieurs success stories qui ont donné aux restaurants des atouts essentiels dans le monde d'aujourd'hui, tourné plus que jamais vers la culture culinaire.

par Blacksheep

Une agence de design internationale, basée à Londres et ayant gagné de nombreux prix. Elle est spécialisée dans la restauration et le monde alimentaire.

PREFACIO

La comida y la bebida siempre han sido aspectos esenciales de la vida; pero, en años recientes, la cultura que las rodea ha vivido una explosión. El sector de la comida y la bebida ha acudido a llenar el vacío dejado por la progresiva migración de las tiendas al mundo de internet, y salir a comer o a cenar se ha convertido en la actividad de ocio favorita de mucha gente. Nunca antes nos habíamos preocupado tanto por lo que comemos y bebemos y por los sitios donde lo hacemos. Se celebran festivales dedicados exclusivamente al arte de preparar el mejor café y podemos degustar un plato de un chef premiado con estrellas Michelin en un aeropuerto antes de tomar un vuelo. Si te descuidas un segundo, te perderás el último concepto de comida callejera. La cantidad de opciones que han surgido para proveer este mercado hambriento es impresionante.

Esta competitividad sin precedentes del mercado ha ido acompañada por un cambio en la percepción de lo que debe ser una buena salida nocturna. Salir a comer y de copas significó en otros tiempos una buena cena y todos los lujosos reclamos que la acompañaban. Hoy, el valor y el prestigio social forman parte de la experiencia.

En el esfuerzo por ofrecer vivencias aún más sorprendentes, el mundo de la comida y la bebida se fusiona y colabora continuamente con sectores como el arte, el diseño, la tecnología y el entretenimiento, y los límites entre todos ellos se difuminan cada vez más. Empresas que nunca se habían relacionado con la comida y la bebida participan cada vez más en esta industria, de maneras inesperadas.

Entre esta explosión de canales y esta abundancia de experiencias, los comensales se han vuelto más exigentes. Han viajado y han comido bien, saben qué es un buen kimchi y cómo se sirve. Han probado burritos en un puesto callejero en México o han visitado una auténtica heladería italiana. Esperan un estándar de calidad y saben reconocerlo, y son capaces de oler y saborear la falta de autenticidad a una milla de distancia.

Cualquier marca que desee encontrar su lugar dentro de este mercado tan fraccionado y competitivo debe trabajar más que nunca. Como diseñadores, nuestro cometido es mejorar la vida de las personas ofreciéndoles una experiencia memorable. Crear esta experiencia significa pensar en todos los puntos de contacto con el cliente.

Las buenas marcas tienen valores, comportamientos e historias que son claros. El branding y el diseño de interiores trasladan estos elementos al ambiente de un espacio y a la claridad y la consistencia de la experiencia del cliente. Lograr estos objetivos exige ir más allá del espacio físico. Servicio de mesa, uniformes, estilo del servicio y hasta el modo en que se comunican los miembros del personal: todo ello debe estar relacionado con lo que se sirve en el plato.

Pero el valor del buen diseño no termina con la oferta de una experiencia memorable para el cliente. Ya se trate de mantener a la gente en sus asientos mediante una disposición inteligente del espacio o de mejorar la permanecia de los empleados creando un entorno en el que se sientan orgullosos de trabajar, el buen diseño es una poderosa herramienta para las empresas. En un mercado tan competitivo, puede dar la ventaja a los restaurantes modernos.

Nuestro estudio siempre aborda los proyectos buscando el espíritu de la marca y la experiencia del cliente. Cuando el hotel Marriott County Hall encargó a Blacksheep que trabajara en el Gillray's Steakhouse & Bar del Marriott, fue fácil identificar ese espíritu. El Gillray, llamado así por el célebre caricaturista del siglo XVIII James Gillray y con un menú que presume de ofrecer lo mejor de los productos ingleses, desde el Aberdeen Angus *steak* hasta el lenguado Dover, tenía que brindar una experiencia inglesa hasta la extravagancia, y eso inspiró cada una de las decisiones creativas que se tomaron. Desde el sofá Chesterfield de nueve metros de largo hasta la cubertería de plata Sheffield y las mesas de roble inglés hasta la selección de ilustraciones satíricas de James Gillray, pasando por los menús y la creación de marca, la solución de diseño tiene un carácter global. El menú de bebidas completa la experiencia al ofrecer a los clientes una selección de treinta y nueve de las mejores ginebras inglesas junto a cócteles con nombres como *Death on the Thames* y *Gin Hound*.

Hoy más que nunca, un buen producto es sólo uno de los aspectos de la experiencia de comer y beber. Con el fin de inspirar fidelidad y preferencia, una identidad visual que refleje perfectamente la filosofía culinaria de un bar o de un restaurante conseguirá que el establecimiento destaque. *Eat & Stay* muestra precisamente estas historias de éxito. En las páginas siguientes se perfilan soluciones notables de branding y diseño de interiores de todo el mundo que han proporcionado a los restaurantes las cualidades únicas que exige la explosión de la cultura de la comida en nuestros días.

de Blacksheep

Agencia internacional independiente y premiada radicada en Londres y especializada en el sector de la comida y la bebida.

PROJECTS

📍 Location

📞 Reservation

🍴 Operating Hours

🚩 Open Time

Mikôto Japanese Cuisine

Design Agency / ADDA Studio & Hochburg   **Creative Director** / Christian Vögtlin
Designer / Christian Vögtlin & Nadine März   **Photographer** / Melanie März

Tübinger Strasse 41 70178 Stuttgart, Germany

0711-5043-2203

Mon – Fri: 12:00 – 15:00, 17:00 – 24:00;
Sat: 12:00 – 24:00; Sun: 17:00 – 23:00

Since 2014

The new Japanese restaurant Mikôto invites consumers to excurse a world of Japanese delicacies full of exciting contrasts and surprising harmonies. To achieve the goal of capturing the essence of Mikôto in the design, ADDA implemented the restaurant with an authentic Japanese concept. The mix of Shodo, the art of Japanese calligraphy, and golden lettering of Mikôto interprets Japanese culture in a modern way.
To achieve luxurious and sophisticated style as well as modern elegance and simplicity, ADDA and Hochburg collaborated on developing a cubic grid that winds its way through the entire concept, bringing it together: from print and digital through to the shelving system of the interior design. The design is a statement for the restaurant: "there is so much more than just sushi."

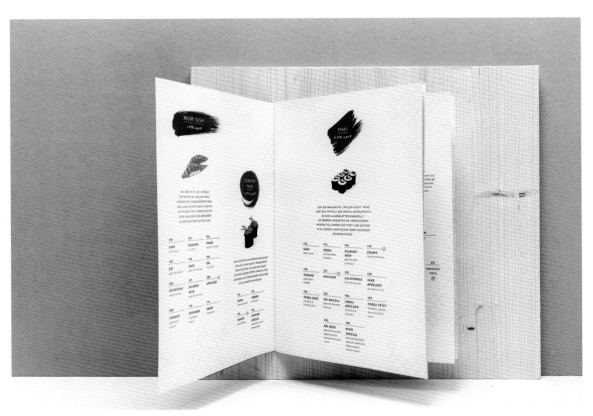

Puebla 109

Design Agency / Savvy Studio
Director / Rafael Prieto
Copywriter / Raul Salazar
Art Work / Marcos Castro, Lucía
Oceguera, Juan Caloca & Luis Alberú

Art Director / Eduardo Hernandez
Designer / Eduardo Hernandez & Bernardo Dominguez
Interior Designer / Marcela Lugo & Arthro Dib
Photographer / Coke Bartrina

📍 Puebla 109, col. North Rome, Mexico City, Mexico

📞 55-6389-7333

🍴 Tue – Sat: 13:00 – 02:00; Sun: 13:00 – 18:00; Closed on Monday

▶ Since 2013

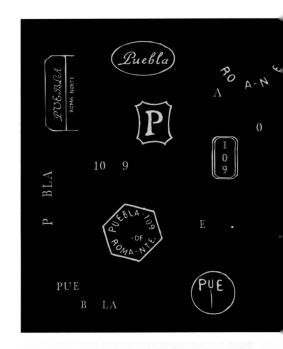

Puebla 109 is a new gastronomic hotspot inside a three–floored 20th century townhouse where art, design, and gastronomy converge. In the morning the place can be used as a work hub while the space evolves and offers food and beverage in the rest of the day. The identity for Puebla 109 was developed around several symbols which draw inspiration from the classic age of Mexican philately. Each symbol works independently but at the same time shares an equal hierarchy and makes up the graphic system with the rest of the symbols. Unlike a more traditional approach to branding, there is no one symbol that bears the weight of the entire brand's identity.

The applications are constructed upon basic or more industrial materials. They are contrasted with bold colors and classic typefaces that have a strong national character, together with a few other graphic elements which resemble those used by the postal service in the past, therefore alluding to the journey that an object undertakes before reaching its final destination.

MIXOLOGÍA_ B1

PUEBLA 109
ROMA NORTE DF

Lillet blanco, Amaro Averna y bitters de café,
añejado en casa en barrica de roble blanco
americano servido con una esfera de hielo.

C04_ Bloody Mary | Infusión de vodka
Ketel One con vegetales, jugo de tomate y
limón, acompañado de un dip de rábanos,
pepinillos y aceitunas rellenas de blue cheese.

$120

109

31

PUEBLA · 109
OF
ROMA · NTE.

Franco

Design Agency / Futura
Photographer / Futura

📍 Av 5 de Febrero #412 | Col Parque Industrial
Jurica, Queretaro 76120, Mexico

📞 +(52)442 218 0621

🍴 Mon – Tue: 08:00 – 18:00;
Wed – Fri: 08:00 – 23:45;
Sun: 09:00 – 18:00;
Sat: 09:00 – 23:45

▶ Since 2013

The identity solution by Futura intends to be
as clear and minimalism as the restaurant
environment. Its constancy goes through the
materials and typographic applications instead of a
single logotype. The location and interior together
with graphic design perfectly connects the urban
and cosmopolitan spirit of the brand.

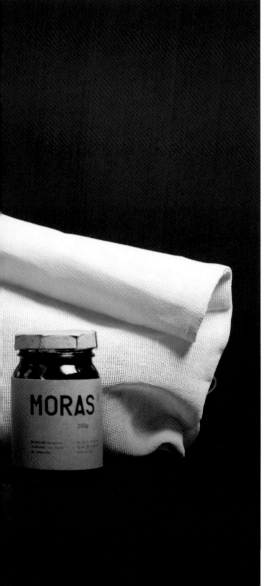

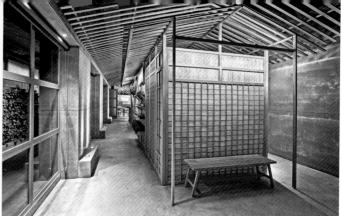

Nozomi
Sushi Bar

Design Agency / Masquespacio
Creative Junior / Nuria Martínez
Graphic Junior / Jairo Pérez & Ana Diaz
Photographer / David Rodríguez & Carlos Huecas

Creative Director / Ana Hernández
Architect Junior / Virgínia Hinarejos
Construction / Helix

📍 Pedro Tercero el Grande 11,
46005 Valencia, Spain

📞 96-148-77-64

🍽 Wed & Sun: 20:30 – 23:30;
Thu – Sat: 13:30 – 16:00,
20:30 – 23:30;
Closed on
Monday & Tuesday

🚩 Since December, 2014

Nozomi Sushi Bar is a high–end Japanese restaurant serving authentic traditional sushi to merely 6 guests. The identified and dual brand name, "Nozomi," presents consistently two values through the whole project: "rational contemporary" and "emotional classic." Masquespacio conveys this duality to consumers through the Western typography as "rational contemporary," while the hiragana (Japanese writing) shows "emotional classic" touch in its logo.

Moreover, Masquespacio fused "rational contemporary" and "emotional classic" into the environment more intensely by the pure state of concrete and grays. "Rational contemporary" is mainly presented within the most structural parts such as walls, ceilings, and floors, while "emotional classis" is linked to the carpentry due to its hand finishes and the warmth of natural wood.

On the aesthetic level, Masquespacio reinterpreted on a metaphoric way of the most authentic Japanese streets through different modules, traduced here into a market, pharmacy, and doors and windows. The rooftops as well communicates the most contemporary and rational part with a clearly Japanese inclination. Meanwhile, up on the roof, cherry–tree's flowers, whose shape was inspired by Origami, bloom naturally. At the first sight when consumers enter the environment, they are brought to a lively Japanese street.

The Newmans' Eat Dine & Whisky

Design Agency / Parametro Studio

📍 Amazonas 234, Colonia del Valle, Del Valle,
66220 San Pedro Garza García, N.L., Mexico

📞 +52 81 2139 8830

🍴 Mon – Thu: 13:00 – 01:00
Fri – Sat: 13:00 – 02:00
Sun: 13:00 – 19:00

▶ Since 2015

Located in the heart of San Pedro Garza Garcia, Mexico, The Newmans' Eat Dine & Whisky is a restaurant–bar characterized by whisky. The task was to develop a brand to celebrate whisky's tradition and expensive taste. The brand starts with a series of three main logotypes, coupled with a strong identity with condensed serif typefaces, and a range of colors that include olive green and red accents. Items such as black and white pictures in the stationary are served to emphasize the tradition and modernity of masculinity.

023

The Pelican
Seafood Bar & Grill

Design Agency / Foreign Policy Design Group
Creative Director / Yah–Leng Yu
Art Director / Yah–Leng Yu
Designer / May Lim

📍 1 Fullerton Road, One Fullerton, #01-01,
Singapore 049213

📞 +65 6438 0400

🍴 Mon – Fri: 12:00 – 15:00, 18:00 – 23:00;
Sat: 12:00 – 23:00; Closed on Sunday

▶ Since January, 2013

Delivering comfort and celebratory spirit as the seafarers, The Pelican is a multipurpose hospitality spot of sea–food restaurant, groovy bar, and club and wine. Inspired by its dual functions, Foreign Policy Design Group developed an illustrative visual identity. The sophisticated illustrations introduce an imaginary and fantastic world where human interact with sea–animals, leading to a graphical context of blurring the boundary between real and imaginary. The same design intent is communicated within the interior space design through the neon pink sea–horse sporting a diver's mask or singular tear–drop light fixtures suspended in air.

WATER

FIJI
SAN PELLEGRINO

SODAS & JUICES

FEVER-TREE TONIC, GINGER BEER
GINGER ALE

COKE, DIET COKE, SPRITE, ROO...

REDBULL, REDBULL SUGAR FR...

ORANGE, PINEAPPLE, APPLE...

BEER

	Bottle
	16
JUKUSEN - ASAHI	
Lager	16
HOEGAARDEN (DRAUGHT)	
Weissbier	
	10
DEAD PONY CLUB	
BY BREW DOG	
Pale ale	16
CARLSBERG	12

1 Fullerton Road, #01-01, One Fullerton
Singapore 049214

www.thepelican.com.sg
t 6536 8229 | f 6536 0954

RESERVATIONS
6438 0400 | enquiry@thepelican.com.sg

THE PELICAN
THE

THE

SEAF

In the grand age of navigation, sightin
with that, a ho
Today, we are inspired to recreate that sam
and old ones renewed with good food and n
the oceans have to offer and embraces time

SALADS

THE PELICAN CRAB LOUIS
asparagus, crabmeat, zippy sauce
18

SMOKED HADDOCK & GREEN BEAN
ratte potato, grapefruit, pepper
18

CHOPPED 'BEACH' SALAD
tomato, cucumber, olive, feta, grilled bread.
pomegranate
14

CRUMBLED BLEU COBB
tomato, bacon, avocado, chopped egg
14

SOUPS

THE PELICAN CRAB LOUIS
asparagus, crabmeat, zippy sauce
18

SMOKED HADDOCK & GREEN BEAN
ratte potato, grapefruit, pepper
18

SMALL PLATE

RHODE ISLAND FRIED SQUID
green olive, capers, banana peppers
18

BLACK PEPPERED CANDIED BACON
brown sugar, lime
14

THE PELICAN POTTED PRAWNS
pimento, pernod, pumpernickel
14

COD'S TONGUE CASSEROLE
roast garlic, pork scratchings
26

OLD FASHIONED CRAB CAKES
quick pickle slaw
22

POTATO & SALT COD MASH
warm tomato vinaigrette
16

RAW

THE PELICAN PLATTE
daily selection of raw oysters & ᴇ
steamed whole lobster, crab & praw
marinated conch salad
99
(Serves 2-3)

OYSTERS
freshly shucked
Market Price
(Served by the half dozen)

THE DAILY CATCH

Check out our specials for
more fresh seafood.

WOODFIRE GRILL

RED BREAM FILLET
anchovy jam
42

SKATE WING CHOP
burnt lemon butter
32

LINE-CAUGHT SWORDFISH STEAK
fresh herb vinaigrette
36

SEA-BRINED BABY CHICKEN
gooseberry relish
32

ANGUS BEEF RIBEYE CAP
whisky mustard
58

COLORADO LAMB CHOPS
peas, apricot, mint
78

RHODE IS
green olive,

BLACK PEPPER
brown

THE PEL

LICAN
GRILL

...seafarers that land was near and
...d ones.

...can, where new bonds are made
...responsibly source the best that
...that honor the daily catch.

OTHERS

EGGPLANT PARCEL (V)
mushroom, crisp cheese
24

ATLANTIC LINGUINI & CLAMS
garlic, chilli flakes, white wine
32

BAKED SNAPPER PIE
fish stew, vegetables, puff pastry
36

CORNFLAKE CRUSTED SCALLOPS
sweet & sour shallots
48

SIDES

STEAMED ASPARAGUS
sea salt, garlic oil
12

ROCKET SALAD
citrus dressing
12

GRILLED CORN
milk cheese, chilli
12

TED POTATO
butter

FRIES

SQUID
ppers

ACON

DRINKS
MENU

DRINKS
MENU

Céltorony

Graphic Designer / kissmiklos
Interior Designer / kissmiklos, Gabor Szego & Andras Hitka
Art Director / kissmiklos
Photographer / Áron Erdőháti

Meder street to 12th, Budapest, Hungary

+36309198979

Mon – Fri 11:00 – 23:00;
Sat – Sun: 15:00 – 23:00
Closed on Monday

since 2015

Céltorony lies in the very base of Népsziget next to
the Danube River, intertwined with the kayaking club.
The logo was designed based on the concept that
people usually watch winners entering the finish line
in water contests in the past. Likewise, the rowers and
cyclists berthing here give it the name a Sport Bistro.
Céltorony welcomes guests with the passion for water
sports or an enthusiasm for the atmosphere of the
bank of the Danube.

SPORTBISZTRÓ
CÉLTORONY

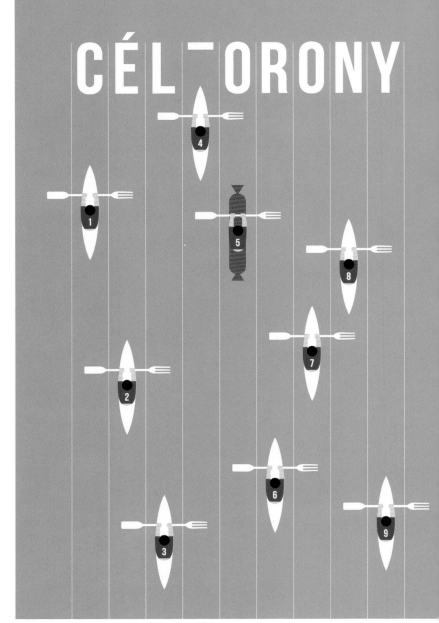

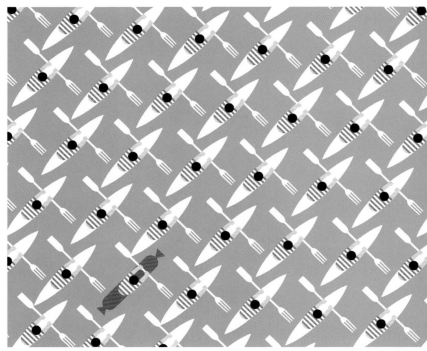

PISILÉS
KÉZMOSÁ
VISZLÁT

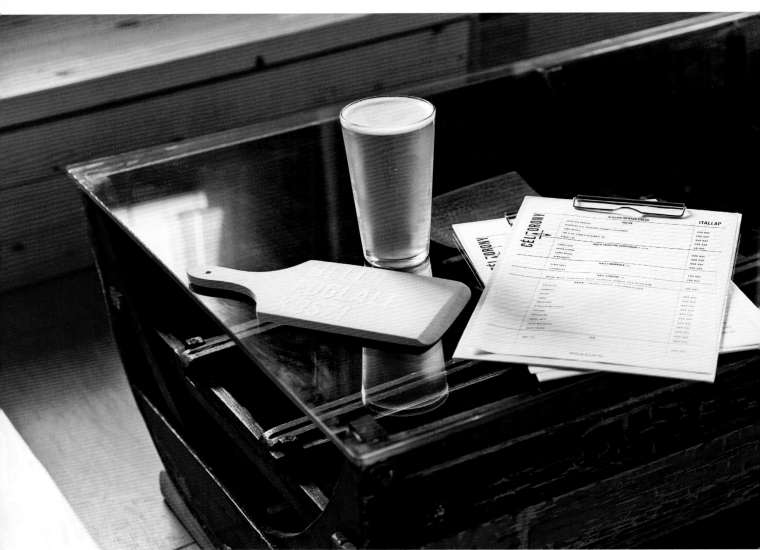

MOSDÓ

"We have to talk about liberating minds as well as liberating society."

enfant terrible, Bar & Café

Design Agency / Studio Eusebio
Art Director / Luca Eusebio
Type Designer / Marc Rudin

Creative Director / Luca Eusebio
Designer / Luca Eusebio & Marc Rudin
Web Designer / Giorgio Favotto

Zentralstrasse 156, 8003 Zürich, Switzerland

+41 (0) 44 461 00 37

Tues – Sat: 17.00 – 24.00;
Closed on Sunday & Monday

Since 2014

enfant terrible, Bar & Café is a restaurant with a musical bent, specifically jazz and hip–hop. Projected to represent their musical, social, and political position with an unconventional and extending visual concept, Studio Eusebio created a logo based on the shape of an octagon, which derives from the the bar room with its 45–degree angled floor plan. The upright italic geometric font, which was inspired by a kind of 45–degree historical hand writing and a utilitarian monospace type, is specially revised for this project. On the menu cover as well as inside the restaurant, the rasterized human images with an octagonal pattern reiterate the concept "enfant terrible."

Bier

Herrgöttli Bier Paul 01	2,0 dl	3.50
Bier Paul 01	3,0 dl	4.50
Bier Paul 02, Flasche	3,3 dl	6.00
Quöllfrisch Naturtrüb Bügel	5,0 dl	7.00
Bier Paul 08 Weizen	5,0 dl	8.00
Super Bock	3,3 dl	6.00
Rothaus Tannenzäpfle Pils	3,3 dl	6.50
Stadtguet Amber	3,3 dl	7.00

Wein

Rotwein
Rame	1,0 dl	5.00
Negro Amaro	1,0 dl	6.50
Martinet Bru	1,0 dl	7.50

Weisswein
Tannu	1,0 dl	5.00
Pecora	1,0 dl	5.50
Sartarelli Classico	1,0 dl	6.50

Schaumwein
Gtera Frizzante	1,0 dl	7.00
Cava	1,0 dl	9.00

Alle Preise verstehen sich in Schweizer Franken inklusive 8% MwSt

Aperitiv

Dolin Vermouth Blanc 16%	4 cl	7.00
Dolin Vermouth Rouge 16%	4 cl	7.00
Campari 23%	4 cl	7.00
Campari Orange/Soda	2 dl	9.00
Aperol Spritz	2,5 dl	12.00
Gespritzter Weisswein	2,5 dl	7.50

Pastis

Ricard 45%	2 cl	7.00
Janot 45%	2 cl	8.00
Pastis HB Henri Bardouin 45%	2 cl	8.00

Digestiv

Grappa di Amarone 40%	2 cl	9.00
Grappa di Barolo 45%	2 cl	11.00
Hennessy Cognac US 40%	2 cl	13.00
Lepanto Solera Brandy 36%	2 cl	13.00
Braulio Amaro Alpino 21%	4 cl	7.00
Fernet Branca 39%	4 cl	9.00

Alle Preise verstehen sich in Schweizer Franken inklusive 8% MwSt

good to
how to
but it's
rous to
how to read
ot how to
pret what
e reading."

"We have to
talk about
liberating
minds as
well as
liberating
society."

ch öppä
y Potter
ribä
was?»

enfant terrible

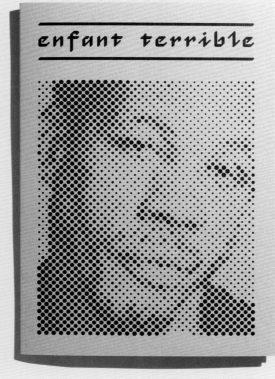

«Les conneries,
c'est le propre
de la jeunesse.
On a besoin
de se brûler
tout seul pour
apprendre.»

"I don't feel like I need to preach to the world or nothing like that. I just feel like I share what I say, and if listeners get it, they get it. And I never underestimate the audience's ability to feel me."

"La palab
describe
mundo no
mundo.»

gäge d bärge
gäge d bärge
gäge d bärge
gäge d bärge
singeni aa
die tüe nume
unestaa

«Penso di
più intel
della nor
na giuro
non mi in
dimostran

Mantra Raw Vegan

Design Agency / Supercake Srl   **Copywriter** / Ideificio
Illustrator / Paola Antòn Vasquez   **Photographer** / Valerio Gavana
Construction Design Team / Mediterranea Costruzioni Srl

Via Panfilo Castaldi 21, 20124
Milano, Italy

39-02-89058575

Mon – Sat: 10:00 – 24:00;
Closed on Sunday

Since January, 2015

Supercake Srl was commissioned to design for Mantra, the first raw vegan restaurant in Italy. The architectural, graphic design and communication idea was based on a seed, an essence of vegan diet, representing the recycle of life as well as the essence of nourishment and wellness. Simplicity became the guiding principle for the whole project by depriving unnecessary elements and fill in rigor, harmony, and functionality. Four distinct but strongly interrelated "environments" – the raw vegan market, the bar and show–cooking area, the raw lab, and the dinner room – were created to refresh the former place to be young, warm, colorful, elegant, but not formal.

guardate pure
n questa cucina non si cuoce niente

lo yoga
per lo stomaco

sapessi com'è sano
sentirsi "raw vegan"
a milano

la cruda varietà

raw vegan market

Grüner Michel
Vegetarian Restaurant

Design Agency / ADDA Studio & Hochburg
Designer / Christian Vögtlin & Nadine März

Creative Director / Christian Vögtlin
Photographer / Melanie März

📍 Green Michel, Marktplatz 5, 71229 Leonberg, Germany

📞 49-7152-395590

🍴 Tue – Thu: 11:30 – 14:00, 17:00 – 22:30;
Fri: 11:30 – 14:00, 17:00 – 23:30;
Sat: 17:00 – 23:30; Sun: 17:30 – 21:30; Closed on Monday

▶ Since 2015

The most distinguishing character of this restaurant design by ADDA is the elegant hand–drawn writing with its rich variations. It evolves into elegant copper–foiled logo or ink illustrations applied on corporate cards, menus, print collaterals, and wall decorations. Apart from the writing, the delicate plant illustrations in picture frames and on plates help boost a cozy atmosphere. Together with the interior design, these elements converts Grüner Michel into a new gastronomy highlight where warm welcomes guests to dine, chat, and be amazed.

Ask For Luigi

📍 305 Alexander St, Vancouver,
BC V6A 1C4, Canada

📞 +1 604-428-2544

🍴 Tue – Fri: 11:30 – 14:30, 17:30 – 22:30;
Sat: 09:30 – 14:30, 17:30 – 23:00;
Sun: 09:30 – 14:30, 17:30 – 21:30;
Closed on Monday

▶ Since 2014

Design Agency /
Glasfurd & Walker (Branding)
& Ste Marie (Interior)
Creative Director /
Phoebe Glasfurd (Branding)
& Craig Stanghetta (Interior)

Ask for Luigi is an Italian-inspired restaurant specializing in fresh handmade pasta and small plates. Canadian creative agency Glasfurd & Walker and Ste Marie collaborate on fusing a cozy and intimate environment for this restaurant. In creating the identity and branding for the restaurant, Glasfurd & Walker created a custom typeface to play against the whimsical and charming name. The interior design by Ste Marie is a manifestation of an idealized recollection and the sense memory of sharing beautiful simple food with loved ones.

Casa Virginia

Design Agency / Savvy Studio
Interior Design Agency / Habitación 116

📍 116 Monterey Avenue, Colonia Roma,
CP 06700, D.F., Mexico

📞 5207 1813

🍴 Tue – Sat: 13:30 – 17:00, 19:30 – 23:00;
Sun: 13:30 – 18:00;
Closed on Monday

▶ Since 2013

Savvy encompasses Casa Virginia as the easiness and familiarity of eating at home, with the highest quality in its cuisine. The identity was developed as a contemporary reinterpretation of the traditional graphic language that was popular in Mexico during the 1920s. The same philosophy and ideals are reflected upon the graphic applications which, though simple in nature, express an upmost attention to the smallest details – through special finishes such as gold foiling – imitating the chef's meticulous process in her cooking.

El Imparcial

Creative Director / Xavi Martínez
Art Director / Texto
Designer / Xavi Martínez

📍 Calle Duque de Alba, 4, 28012 Madrid, Spain

📞 91 79 58 986

🍴 Mon – Fri: 12:00 to 20:30
Sat & Sun: 11:30 to 20:30
Since 2015

▶ Since 2015

El Imparcial is a restaurant, bar, and concept store in Madrid. Located at the house of a historical editor of newspaper El Imparcial, the restaurant inherits the taste for art, expositions, culture, and food, and aims to rebuild a neighborhood of citizen participation to push towards a renewed creative activity. As a result, the place serves as a restaurant and an exhibition place. The dynamic logo composed of circle and square is therefore created to represent its characteristics and be easy to apply in different occasions and media.

Nos hace mucha ilusión que nos acompañes en la inauguración de el imparcial. Restaurante, bar & concept store.

Se ruega confirmación:
alberto@farrago.com

C/ Duque de Alba, 4
28012 Madrid
(zona Tirso de Molina)

9:30 – 00:00
28.04.2015

el imparcial.

Presentamos assistant magazine Vol II en el imparcial.
(las nucas de Xavier Dolan y Gia Coppola en portada)

El evento se celebrará
en el espacio i.

C/ Duque de Alba, 4
28012 Madrid
(zona Tirso de Molina)

04.05.2015
19:00

el imparcial.

23 de abril

Sant Jordi en el imparcial. Los libros nos afectan al 5%

en el día del libro
nuestras rosas se
llaman margaritas

C/ Duque de Alba, 4
28012 Madrid
(zona Tirso de Molina)

23.04.2015
9:30 – 00:00

el imparcial.

"De lo que no
se puede hablar,
hay que callar."

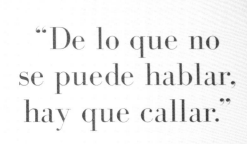

Ninigi

Design Agency / Estudio Yeyé
Photographer / Pato Negro

Designer / Orlando Portillo, Daniel Escorcia & Francisco Leon

📍 Peripheral Youth 3102, Chihuahua, Mexico

📞 01 614 430 1707

🍴 Tue – Wed: 13:30–23:00;
Thu – Sat: 13:30–23:30;
Sun: 13:30–18:00

▶ Since 2014

Estudio Yeyé converted the Japanese mythology of Ninigi, the patron deity of rice, in a project of branding, packaging, furniture design, object design, multimedia, and interior design. Typical Japanese aesthetics, such as simplicity, subtle beauty, and austere grace, are engaged in the branding design and marketing. The interior design recreates an environment where ancient Japan and contemporary elements are mixed in a warm and modern setting.

TEPPAN
YAKI
SUSHI BAR

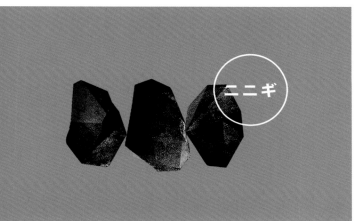

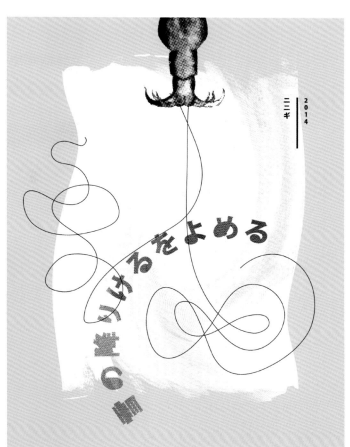

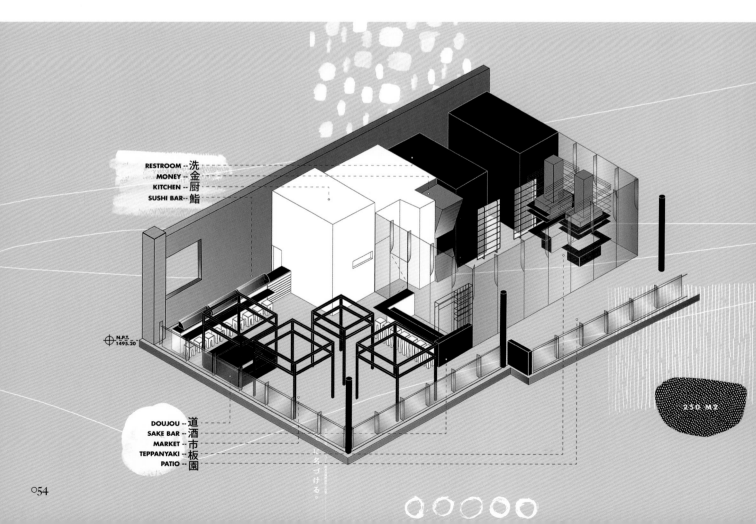

RESTROOM -- 洗
MONEY -- 金
KITCHEN -- 厨
SUSHI BAR -- 鮨

N.P.T.
1495.20

250 M2

DOUJOU -- 道
SAKE BAR -- 酒
MARKET -- 市
TEPPANYAKI -- 板
PATIO -- 園

Lanes of London, Marriott London

Design Agency / Blacksheep
Designer / Tony Duesbury

📍 London Marriott Hotel, 140 Park Ln, London W1K 7AA, the UK

📞 +44 20 7647 5664

🍴 Open daily 06:30 – 23:00

▶ Since 2013

A bespoke pattern and a decorative page border based on the logo elements was developed and implemented across the menus and wider collateral. Halftone, black and white vintage aerial photographs of London boroughs create a vintage feel to the overall impression.

The use of striking beveled mirrors and a variety of clear and colored glass at the bar reflect the marriage between the classical and contemporary design. The glamorous mirrored chimney breast and elegant fireplace provide a warm welcome to guests.

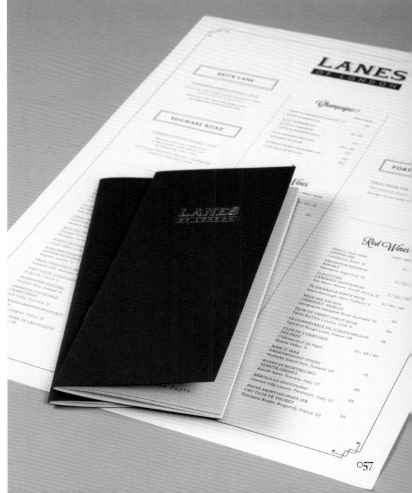

Set Cafè

Design Agency / Enserio

⦿ Passeig Darder 55, 17820, Banyoles, Spain

📞 +34 668 57 07 04

⚑ Since 2014

Enserio took up the graphic design for this restaurant located next to Banyoles lake, where the food is made of natural and local products. A fresh logo was therefore created with the combination of a potato print font, the Patata Condensed, and artful food illustrations to deliver the concept. Furthermore, the large plains of light colors on coasters as well as inside the space help promote the airy and fresh atmosphere.

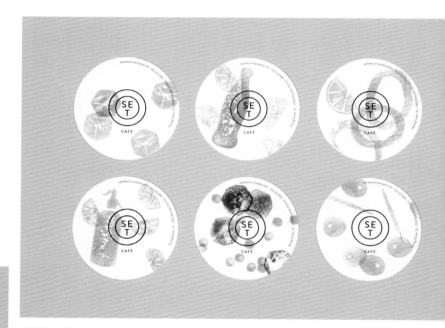

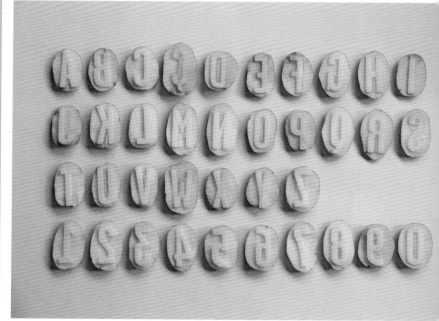

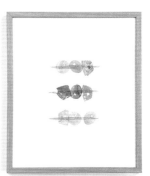

AL SET
I AL LLIT
EL PRIMER
CRIT

ON
MENGEN
DOS
MENGEN
SET

Restaurant Vora Estany

Design Agency / Enserio

📍 Passeig Darder 55, 17820, Banyoles, Spain

📞 +34 972 57 63 53

🍴 Mon – Thu: 07:30 – 22:00;
Fri & Sat: 07:30 – 24:00;
Sun: 08:00 – 21:00

▶ Since 2013

The identity for the Restaurant Vora Estany is based on a combination of a powerful and abstract symbol with illustrations made by pen. The sum of these ideas is converted into an exercise in creativity with infinite possibilities, which give an obvious richness to a graphic that in itself is relatively corporate. The pen becomes the main character of the graphic to the point that even the cursor of the website traces its own path. Enserio created a lively graphic image, with a touch of humor for a dynamic restaurant.

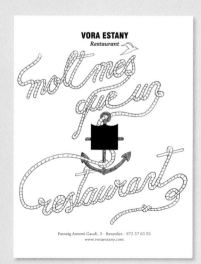

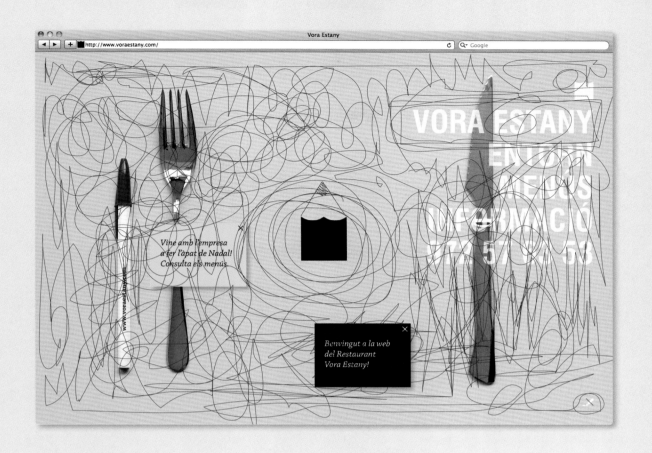

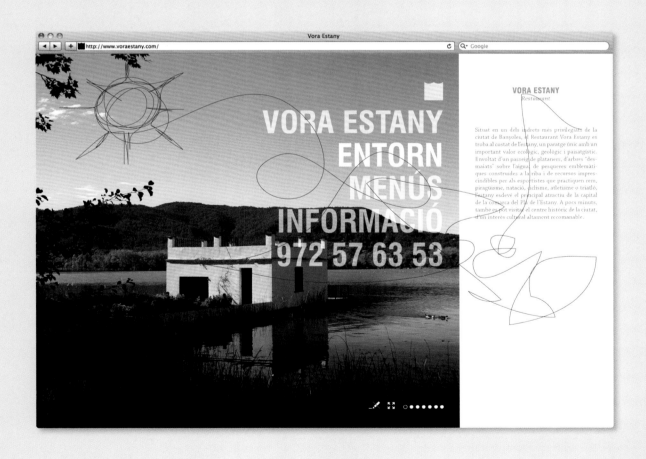

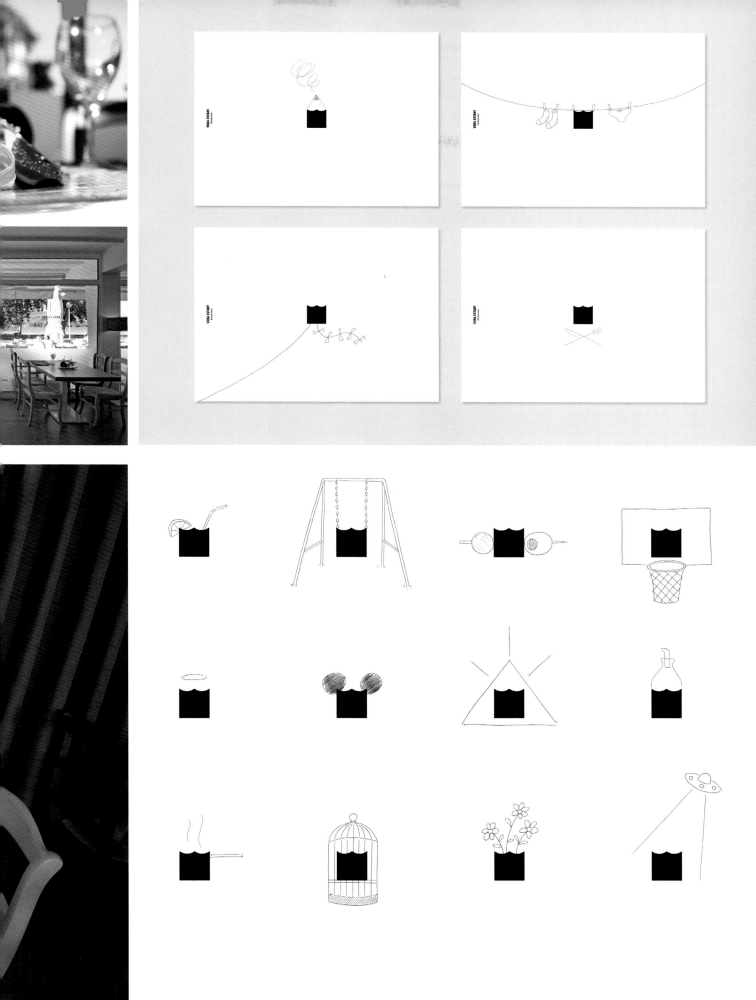

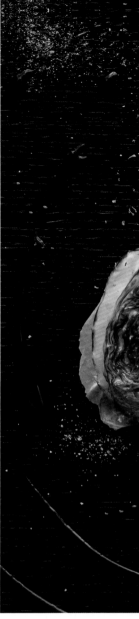

BA 53

Designer / Nicklas Haslestad
Producer / Anders Gottlieb–Nygaard
Photographer / Marte Garmann

Bygdoy Alle 53, 0265 Oslo, Norway

+47 21 42 05 90

Bar
Mon – Wed: 16:00 – 24:00;
Thu – Sat: 16:00 – 01:00;
Close on Sunday

Since 2015

The identity of BA 53 is inspired by the pride building "Bygdøy Allé 53" and the iconic street signs in Oslo. Nicklas and his team created an identity rooted in history, yet representative for a young generation of hungry cooks. Their goal was to create an identity that reflects freshness and purity alongside with tradition and history. The menu of BA 53 changes in pace with the Nordic seasons and the color scheme is converted accordingly. In addition to a genuine story behind the name and origin, the challenge was to merge this with the innovative chef style of BA 53.

Velkommen til vårt nye restauranthus
BA 53 – i historiske Bygdøy Allé 53.
Restaurant, bar, kaffebar og chambre
séparée. Lekent og litt røft. Jordnært,
ærlig og veldig godt. Kom innom for en
morgenkaffe, en cocktail i baren eller
en smaksrik middag med en god flaske vin.

B   A
53

booking@ba53.no
+47 214 20 590
www.ba53.no

Adresse
Bygdøy Allé 53
0265 Oslo

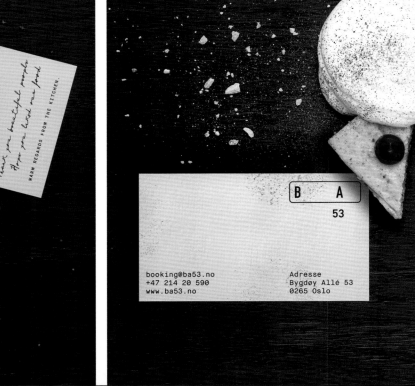

WARM REGARDS FROM THE KITCHEN.

B   A
53

booking@ba53.no
+47 214 20 590
www.ba53.no

Adresse
Bygdøy Allé 53
0265 Oslo

nr: II

GAVEKORT

Til   Kari

Fra   Hans

Verdi   One Thousand Five Hundred

Gavekortet må løses
inn 6 måneder etter
APR 2.5 2013

Booking
booking@ba53.no
+47 21 42 05 90

www.ba53.no

Adresse
Bygdøy Allé 53
0265 Oslo

Simple

Design Agency / Brandon
Director / Boris Alexandrov & Anna Domovesova
Designer / Olga Novihava,
Elena Parhisenko & Anton Storozhev
Illustrator / Alexandr Osipenko
Copywriter / Dimitry Panasjuk
Interior Designer /
Anna Domovesova
Visualization / Nikolay Mihov
Photographer / Andrey Shalimov & Yana Korobenko

📍 Saksahanskoho St, 102, Kiev, Ukraine

📞 +380 44 288 0808

🍴 Open daily 08:00–22:00

▶ Since 2014

Kiev based restaurant Simple concentrates on offering fresh food made of local ingredients. The entire design includes not just common standards for logo, colors, fonts, and pattern application, but also the naming and more. Brandon empowers it with simplicity in the matter of design by a friendly attitude with a human face and communications. Under a strict guideline, Brandon developed several sets of icons, illustrations, the detailed description on communication usage, game sets, stickers, a few types of menu, and etc. Poster, being a visual delight for guests, communicates a cross–cutting theme. This solution focuses on the main idea of the restaurant: making interesting and tasty dishes out of basic and local materials.

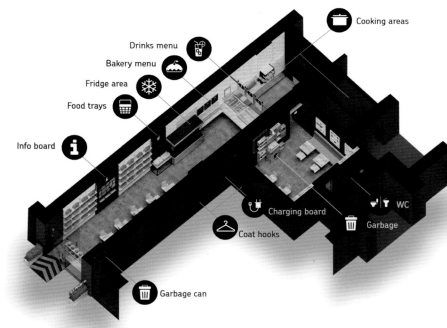

The Gorgeous Kitchen

Design Agency / Blacksheep
Designer / Amy Wenden

📍 Heathrow, Terminal 2, Airside
Departures, Level 5, London, the UK

📞 +44 (0)7795 636840

🍴 5 am to last departing flight

⌖ Since 2014

Set within the fast paced airport environment of Heathrow, The Gorgeous Kitchen was created as an escape into a world of tranquility. A collaboration between four female chef's, the design embraces a modern essence of femininity; welcoming yet refined and with a touch of the ethereal.

Taking inspiration from the formation of a rockpool, Blacksheep's approach meant the seating arrangements provide an unhindered space, giving an overall feeling of tranquility. Delicate copper vinaigrettes connect the spaces from a central point, creating pockets of natural rest for guests. Antique Murano glass shades further complement this calm atmosphere.

Park Restaurant + Distillery

Branding Design Agency / Glasfurd & Walker
Creative Director / Phoebe Glasfurd
Designer / Phoebe Glasfurd

📍 219 Banff Ave, Banff, AB T1L, Canada

📞 +1 403-762-5114

🍴 Open daily 11:00–01:00

▶ Since 2015

Inspired by the outdoors and the love of the National Park itself, Park is a restaurant that celebrates Banff's alpine history and lifestyle. Park is a place both locals and visitors can experience something true and genuine to Banff, both in design and in the food served. It is a place that honors history in a modern, yet rustic setting that features "campfire cooking" inspired food and house–made spirits.

The packaging for the spirits celebrate the natural beauty of Banff – each spirit type is represented by illustrations of iconic mountains in the Banff National Park – depicted in color tones complimentary to the product flavor.

E CAMPFIRE IS THE ORIGINAL RESTAURANT. A
ACE WHERE PEOPLE GATHERED TOGETHER TO EAT,
INK AND LAUGH ABOUT THE ONE THAT GOT AWAY.
WAS HUGE. YOU SHOULD HAVE SEEN IT. THAT'S
HY FIRE IS AT THE HEART OF PARK. BECAUSE OUR
AVINGS FOR FOODS COOKED THAT WAY RUN DEEP.
OD-FIRED. SPIT-ROASTED. SMOKEY-SAVOURY. AND
TOP IT ALL OFF, WE INFUSE, MARINATE AND
ERALLY ENHANCE USING SPIRITS WE DISTILL
RSELVES FROM THE BEST INGREDIENTS ON EARTH.
WELCOME TO PARK. GATHER 'ROUND.

BREAKFAST

LUNCH & DINNER

DISTILLER & THE CHEESE

MADE FOR SHARING
Served with pretzel bread, kitchen pickles,
and fixins' add cured meats - 18

FLAMING RACLETTE
An apres must - 21

WHISKEY EMMENTAL FONDUE
Swiss guides specialty potato salad, coleslaw, cornbread - 29.75

APPS + SNACKS

ADD A PAN OF
CORNBREAD TO THE TABLE
Maple rum butter - 6.50

TRAIL MIX
Nuts, this, that - 5

LEGEND

ROTISSERIE CHICKEN CHOWDER
Roasted corn, bacon, corn bread croutons - 10

= WOOD FIRED
ROTISSERIE GRILL

CALAMARI
Tomato butter, dill aioli, lemon - 16.75

= MADE WITH BOOZE

SPIT ROASTED WINGS
Korean bbq, park hot sauce, kimchi - 15.75

= GLUTEN FREE

LOBSTER ROLLS
Lemon herb aioli, butterleaf, butter bun - 17.50

= VEGETARIAN

DIRTY FRIES
Baked beans, odd bits, cheese curds - 13.75

SHRIMP HUSHPUPPIES
Buttermilk ranch for dippin - 12.75

FOOD SOURCE

KALE & GRITS
Pine nuts, garlic, reggiano - 14

ALBERTA BORN
& RAISED

CORNFLAKE PULLED PORK FINGERS
Maple whisky & bacon dipping sauce - 15.75

OCEAN WISE

CAMPFIRE FLATBREAD
Fresh mozza, tomatoes, garlic, basil - 15.75

OKANAGAN CHERRY
WOOD & MESQUITE

CHEFS BOURBON
BBQ SAUCE

Bord 13

Design Agency / Snask
Artist / Emilie Florin

Art Director / Magdalena Czarnecki
Photographer / Gustav Arnetz

Engelbrektsgatan 13, 211 33 Malmö, Sweden

+46 42 587 88

Tue – Thu: 17:30 – 24:00;
Fri & Sat: 17:30 – 01:00;
Closed on Sunday & Monday

Since 2015

Sweden design agency Snask helped Bord 13 with concept and naming, the identity, as well as the whole interior. The name is inspired from the superstition of table 13 (Bord 13 in Swedish), which means bad luck, and the location of the restaurant on street no. 13. In order to present "dark side," Snask created experimental and somewhat morbid illustrations for the concept. The identity, with a monotone, works well as a contrasts to the quite light, Nordic and sober interior of Bord 13.

Época

Design Agency / Estudio Yeyé
Designer / Orlando Portillo, Daniel Escorcia & Francisco Leon

📍 Periférico de la Juventud 3102,
4to piso, plaza 3106

📞 01 614 430 1707

🍴 Tue – Wed: 13:30 – 23:00;
Thu – Sat: 13:30 – 23:30;
Sun: 13:30 – 18:00

▶ Since 2014

The culture of Mexico City in early twentieth century, defined by cultural invasion and mixture of cultural, ideological streams, and Paris fashion with vibrant Mexican popular culture, was cherished and given rebirth by Estudio Yeyé for Época. The team developed corporate identity, interior design, branding, and editorial design. Through the applications, retro illustrations, and glitzy interior design, Época merges modern and classic, treasuring the period of time that left a footprint on the gastronomy of modern Mexico.

Gillray's Steakhouse & Bar

Design Agency / Blacksheep
Designer / Amy Wenden

📍 County Hall, Westminster Bridge Rd,
London SE1 7PB, The UK

📞 020 7902 8000

🍴 Mon – Fri: 06:30-22:30;
Sat & Sun: 07:00-22:30

▶ Since 2012

Blacksheep's concept pays homage to the restaurant's namesake James Gillray, a famed caricaturist of the late eighteenth century, and its most English of locations – the Grade II listed County Hall, built 100 years ago to house London's government.

Driven by this brand personality, the F&B offer showcases the very best of English produce, and the interior design draws inspiration from classic English detailing and materials. From a nine meter long Chesterfield sofa, English oak tabletops and bespoke chandeliers, through to tailored staff uniforms, menus and Sheffield silverware, every touch point speaks to an eccentric English charm.

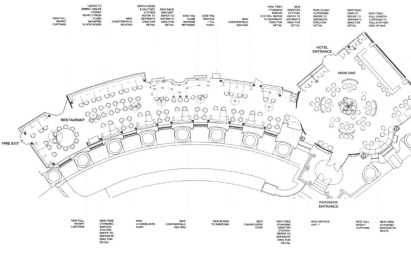

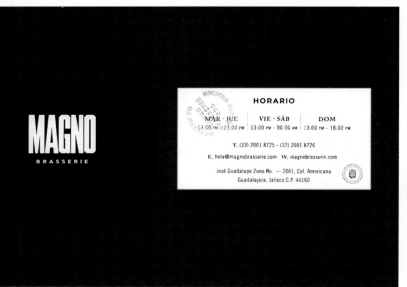

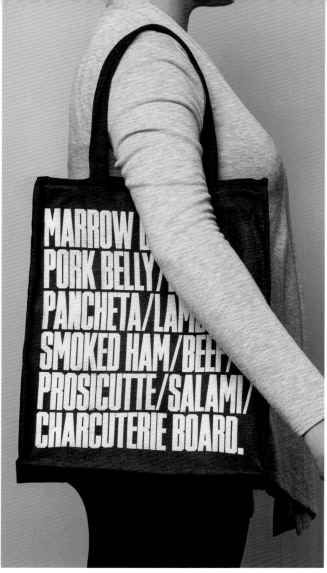

HORARIO

MAR - JUE	VIE - SÁB	DOM
13:00 PM - 23:00 PM	13:00 PM - 00:00 AM	13:00 PM - 18:00 PM

T. (33) 2001 8725 - (33) 2001 8726

E. hola@magnobrasserie.com W. magnobrasserie.com

José Guadalupe Zuno No. — 2061, Col. Americana
Guadalajara, Jalisco C.P. 44160

MAGNO
BRASSERIE

Magno Brasserie

Design Agency / Anagrama

📍 José Guadalupe Zuno #2061 Col. Americana C.P.
44160 Guadalajara, Jalisco, Mexico

📞 (33) 2001 0724

🍴 Tue – Thu: 13:00 – 23:00;
Fri – Sat: 13:00 – 24:00;
Sun: 13:00 – 18:00

▶ Since 2014

Magno Brasserie is a restaurant specializing in Mexican dishes. Located in Guadalajara, Mexico, it states the devotion to serving dishes made of the highest quality of protein.
The visual identity presents a sense of masculinity with rustic and traditional influences, and starts with an impacting typographic logotype with considerable visual weight. The typography unifies the cursive handwriting, giving it an artisan touch. A rustic emblem is added to the stamp, keeping consistency throughout its visual line. The leather and wood applications achieve concept unification, giving the brand an antique aesthetic.

TIMMONS

SLOW ROASTED PORK

GOTHAM

Leaving the bone in adds a bit of extra flavour and having a layer of fat helps to keep the meat nice and moist as it roasts.

CASLON

Preheat your oven to 2 20°C / 425°F / gas 7.

TRADE GOTHIC

2 kg higher-welfare shoulder of pork, bone-in, skin on
sea salt and freshly ground black pepper
2 red onions, halved
2 carrots, peeled and halved lengthways

O'Petit en'K

📍 12 rue Poquelin moliere,
33000, Bordeaux, France

📞 +33 5 56 52 50 16

🍴 Mon – Fri: 09:00 – 16:00;
Closed on weekend

▶ Since 2013

Design Agency /
STUDIO HEKLA
Creative & Art Director /
Kevin Auger & Antoine Gervais
Designer /
Johan Luciano & Thomas Pujol
Photographer /
Julien Fernandez

STUDIO HEKLA was commissioned to the refurbishment of the street food restaurant O'Petit en'K, including graphic and interior challenge to completely rethink street food. The logo, which is reminiscent of both American university sport cockades and New York street culture, was embarked on a proposal of a restaurant of an industrial style with a New York City–like atmosphere. The objective was to create a strong, charismatic, and friendly identity in a small space. The combination of different scales has allowed them to more accurately anticipate the assimilation of communication media and custom made furniture. The space, furniture, and visual identity echo each to form a consistent and coherent whole.

Home Bakery

Design Agency / Blacksheep
Designer / Annette Dennis & Kate McPartland

📍 Al Wasl Rd, Dubai, UAE

📞 +971 4 344 4462

🍴 Sat – Wed: 07:00 – 22:45
Thu – Fri: 07:00 – 24:00

▶ Since 2014

Blacksheep developed a house–like structure within the internal framework of the restaurant, creating an atmosphere of homeliness, warmth, and comfort – the bakery's home.

The word mark was created using a unique set of hand drawn letter forms – the irregularities emphasizing how the desserts themselves are made. Brand mark variations then reference baking in the most literal sense – the sprinkling of cocoa or icing sugar, and the shape of Home Bakery's most infamous product: the Chewy Melt cookie. The colors used, starting from a deep green and growing to peach are taken from the classic ingredient of Arabic baking – the pistachio nut.

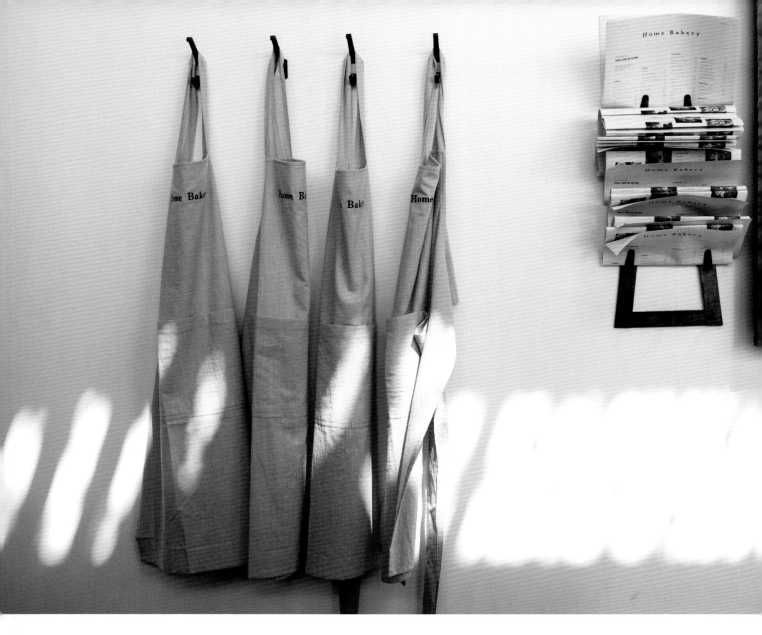

BARBA Restaurant

Branding Designer / Filip Pomykalo, Marita Bonačić & Negra Nigoević
Graphic Designer / Negra Nigoević & Filip Pomykalo
Interior Designer / Marita Bonačić
Photographer / Marita Bonačić

Boskoviceva 5, Dubrovnik 20000, Croatia

+385 91 205 3488

Open daily 10:00–01:00

Since June 2014

BARBA, which is a Dalmatian colloquial expression for uncle, old gentleman, man of the sea, and fisherman, is a place in Dubrovnik, Croatia, where one can experience tradition, local flavors, spices and dishes. The three designers collaborated together in terms of branding and interior design. The logo with an old man's head and the seafaring inspired icons not only connect with its name, but also endow the restaurant with an energetic image to attract younger consumers. This contemporary design approach was used to introduce the fusion of past and present by combining traditional cuisine prepared in a modern manner as well as the visual identity presenting local motives in a modern way.

Krystian's Kitchen

Designer / Paweł Kozakowski
Interior Designer / Kamila Dzionek
Interior Photographer / Yassen Hristov

📍 Ksiazeca 6, Warsaw 00-498, Poland

📞 +(48)22 628 63 45

🍴 Mon - Sat: 09: 00-22: 00;
Sun: 10:00-18:00

▶ Since 2015

Krystian's Kitchen, founded by passionate cooks, is a
simple restaurant offering traditional recipes, which
are drawn from Mediterranean culture. Dishes are
made of the highest quality seasonal ingredients
sourced from local suppliers.

The branding and interior solution, intended to be
as simple as the restaurant's purpose, deliver a clear,
bold, and strong impression to the consumers. As
well, the color palette of red, black, and white is
a strong appeal by keeping a visual consistency
through the whole design.

We serve always

SIMPLY
BUT
DELICIOUS
FOOD

Krystian's
Kitchen

Data, godzina, typ wypieku   Pieczątka

Książęca 6   kontakt@krystianskitchen.pl   krystianskitchen
Śródmieście, Warszawa   tel.: 22 628 63 45   www.krystianskitchen.pl

Krystian's
Kitchen

Krystian's
Kitchen

Artigiano

📍 1 Paternoster Square, City of
London, London EC4M 7DX, the UK

📞 020 72480407

🍴 Mon – Fri: 07: 00 – 21: 00
Sat & Sun: 10:30 – 18:00

▶ Since 2013

Design Agency / POST
Creative Director / Ric Bell

Artigiano offers beautifully crafted espresso coffee, artisan food, fine wines, craft beers, and cocktails. Consumers can grab an espresso during the day, while get indulged in a glass of wine at night. POST were commissioned to develop a visual identity and grow its communications to better reflect this transformation.

They designed a full custom typeface, signage, environmental graphics, iconography, patterns, food and drink packaging along with in–store posters and promotional postcards. Once implemented, POST commissioned a suite of photographs which were used on the dynamically scrolling website.

ARTIGIANO

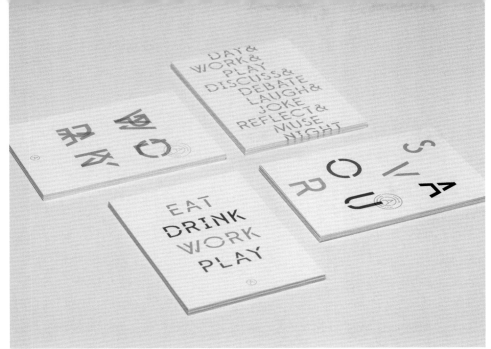

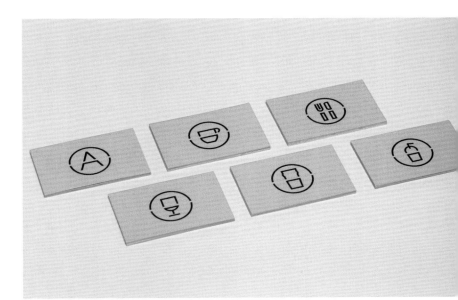

A B C D E F G

H I J K L M N

O P Q R S T U

V W X Y Z

Sean's Kitchen Adelaide

Designer / Gemma Warriner

Sean Connolly is one of the most well-respected chefs in Australia and New Zealand. His latest endeavor is the opening of his first restaurant in Adelaide, South Australia – the aptly named Sean's Kitchen. Inspired by his travels to New York and its vivid food history, the Sean's Kitchen brand represents a space where classic food is transformed into a contemporary atmosphere. The identity reflects this through the contrast of classic new world and old world typefaces whilst the brand collateral brings to life the elegance, origins and roots of food. Sean's vision to create a truly unique experience is extended with items such as Sean's branded retail products and Sean's Kitchen seed packets which allow the consumer to become part of this food journey.

- Station Rd, Adelaide SA 5000, Australia
- +61 8 8218 4244
- Mon – Fri: 11:00 – 24:00
  Sat & Sun: 08:00 – 24:00
- Since 2014

Kaldi Azul

Design Agency / Estudio Yeyé
Designer / Orlando Portillo
Photographer / Villalobos & Bieno Jimenez
Architect / Gerardo Romero

📍 Paseo Simon Bolívar 208 B, Zona
Centro, 31000 Chihuahua, Mexico

📞 +52 614 415 0003

🍴 Open daily 8:00 – 22:00

▶ Since 2014

Kaldi is a café with great emotional attachment.
Together with Gerardo Romero and his architecture
team, Estudio Yeyé made a commercial interior
design project that portrays a very convincing way
the almost religious devotion that has the "kaldianos"
to serving a good cup of coffee.

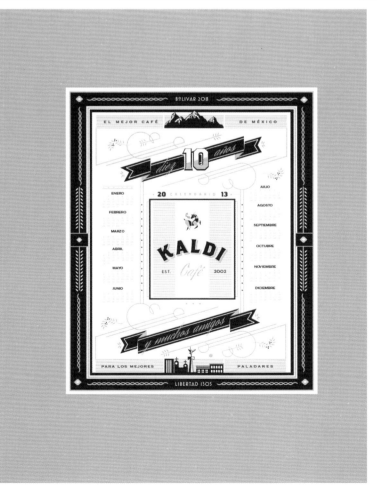

Scheu's Essen & Trinken

Design Agency / ADDA Studio
Director / Janick Neundorf, Michael
Adolph, Nadine März & Thomas Martin

Creative Director / Christian Vögtlin
Website Designer/ Mario Kober
Photographer / Frederik Laux

Bahnhofstraße 6, 71126 Gäufelden, Germany

+49 7032 9196327

Wed – Fri: 17:30 – 22:30;
Sat – Sun: 11:30 – 14:30, 17:30 – 23:00;
Closed on Monday & Tuesday

Since 2014

ADDA Studio's conceptual menu for Scheu, which was established with a fresh restaurant concept, included: interior design, corporate identity, and a fresh website – the agency's favorite menu. In this manner, ADDA Studio brought Scheu's to life in less than two months and with all the trimmings: a harmonious design from a beer mat with fish theme to the copper embossed business cards and an interior design.

Bambudda

Branding Design Agency / Post Projects
Designer / Alex Nelson & Beau House
Photographer / Jennilee Marigomen & Grady Mitchell
Interior Design Agency / Ste Marie

📍 99 Powell Street Vancouver, British
Columbia, V6A 1E9, Canada

📞 (604) 428-0301

🍴 Tue – Sun: 17:30 – 24:00; Closed on Monday

▶ Since 2013

Bambudda is a modern Chinese cuisine restaurant
located in Vancouver's Gastown district. Post
Projects created a visual identity that was applied
to menus, stationery and signage. They also
designed a custom banana leaf wallpaper used
throughout the space.

食
EAT

99 Powell Street
Vancouver
info@bambudda.ca
www.bambudda.ca
604.428.0301

BAMBUDDA

BAMBUDDA
99 POWELL STREET
5:30 - MIDNIGHT, TUESDAY-SUNDAY
CLOSED MONDAYS

飲

DRINK

BAMBUDDA

99 Powell Street
Vancouver
info@bambudda.ca
www.bambudda.ca
604 428 0301

BAMBUDDA

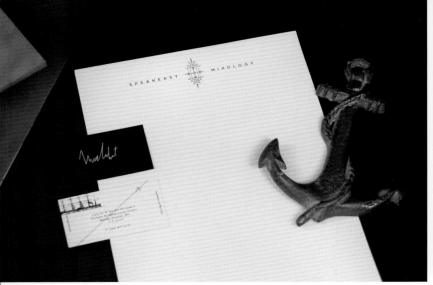

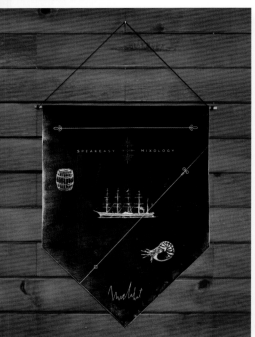

Malahat – Speakeasy & Mixology

Design Agency / Bienal Comunicación
Creative Director / Carlos Martínez Trujillo
Designer / Eugenia Díaz Peon

📍 Parque Santa Lucia Local 2, Calle
55 x 60, Mérida, Yucatán, México

📞 (999) 923 1979

🍴 Wed – Sat: 19:30 – 02:00

▶ Since 2015

Malahat was the name of a historical smuggling boat during the Prohibition. Bienal Comunicación created a handwritten logo, not very legible with a mysterious air. Their purpose was to keep the enigma. The symbol integrating many elements contributes to giving the bar a very unique personality. All the other illustrations were made to complement the story behind the brand. In collaboration with Punto Arquitectónico, they aimed to create a complete and consistent work, a place where the brand and the environment bond nicely together.

GIN GIN MULE

Hendrick's Gin, mint, lime juice, sugar, ginger beer.

$120

OAXACA OLD FASHIONED

Eterno Mezcal, sugar, bitters, orange.

$130

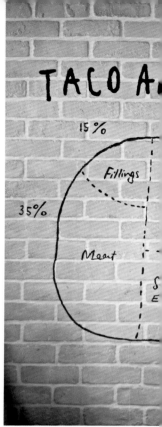

MexOut

📍 39 Pekin St, Singapore 048769

📞 +65 9770 7441

🍴 Mon – Fri: 11:30 – 22:00; Closed on weekend

▶ Since 2013

Design Agency /
Bravo Company
Creative Director /
Edwin Tan
Art Director /
Jasmine Lee
Project Management /
Janice Teo

MexOut is a fresh–mex eatery in Singapore. Imagining MexOut to be a young eccentric Mexican food expert, or "Mex'pert," the shop interior is styled to his living quarters in the basement of his parent's house. As with most eccentric experts, he keeps a wall–of–clues with a Mexican map and pinned locations to track down the freshest ingredients and their suppliers. Being anti–establishment, MexOut does not adopt a proper brand logo but presents it differently every time. About 20 hand–drawn logos were created to be used in rotation. Similarly for the rest of the collaterals, every element was handwritten or hand–drawn with no use of a computer for the creation of any graphics.

My

25%

5%

20%

LIFE'S LIKE A
BURRITO. YOU
HAVE TO FILL
IT UP WITH
THE BEST
INGREDIENTS.

MEXOUT

MEXOUT
39 PEKIN STREET
FAR EAST SQUARE
S'PORE 048769
T: +65 9770 7441
WWW. MEXOUT. COM
OPENS LUNCH
& DINNER

MAKE
SALSA
NOT
WAR.

MEXOUT

THE TACO
CANNON

MEXOUT

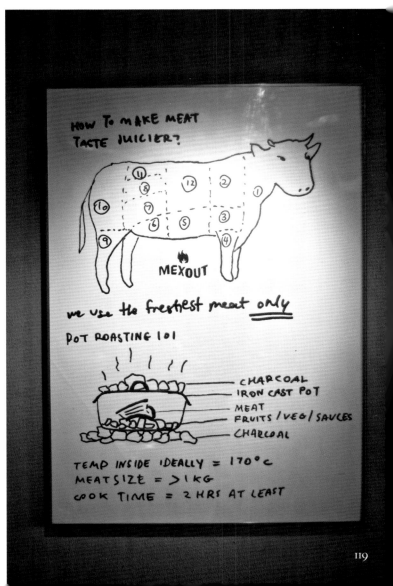

HOW TO MAKE MEAT
TASTE JUICIER?

MEXOUT

we use the freshest meat ONLY

POT ROASTING 101

CHARCOAL
IRON CAST POT
MEAT
FRUITS / VEG / SAUCES
CHARCOAL

TEMP INSIDE IDEALLY = 170°C
MEAT SIZE = >1 KG
COOK TIME = 2 HRS AT LEAST

Allegrezza

Art Director & Designer /
Masaomi Fujita

2-13-8 Ryogoku 130-0026, Sumida-ku, Japan

+81 3-5624-6535

Tue – Sun: 11:30 – 15:00; 18:00 – 23:00
Closed on Monday

Since 2015

Allegrezza is an Italian bar where guests can enjoy many varieties of wine and hors d'oeuvres using seasonal foodstuffs. Being inspired by the Italian shop name meaning "cheerful" and "fun," the designer carried out creating an image of a shop having "circus" as the keyword. The logo depicts a scene where a bear, the star of the circus, returns to a bar after finishing his work. A friendly design was created all the while maintaining an atmosphere of an adult like bar.

イタリアンバール・アレグレッツァ

ADDRESS. 〒224-0041
横浜市都筑区仲町台 1-22-18 プロミネンス2F
TEL. 045-0000 0000
MAIL. allegrezzan4@yahoo.co.jp
Facebook.「アレグレッツァ 仲町台」で検索
www.facebook.com/nn5.nn8.uyk

Local Mbassy

310 Wattle St, Ultimo NSW 2007,
Australia

02 8084 3467

Mon – Fri: 07:00 – 16:00;
Sat – Sun: 08:00 – 16:00

Since 2015

Designer /
Korolos Ibrahim
Graffiti /
Sid Tapia
Photographer /
Shayben Moussa
Fit Out /
David Haines

The Local Mbassy is a boutique café and kitchen paying homage to the locals of the 1920's. Deeply enthused by the Australian prohibition–era, Korolos Ibrahim and his teammates sent salute to the local hooligans, the revolutionaries, and to those who made a difference in moulding up today's Australian art, fashion and coffee culture.

Upon receiving the brief for the undeveloped start–up business, it was fundamental that a full creative direction, business development, concept, brand and design were developed. This was in the hopes of creating a destination store that played a crucial role in Sydney's social and foodie culture while serving the perfect brew of Campos Specialty Coffee.

LOCAL ᴹBASSY

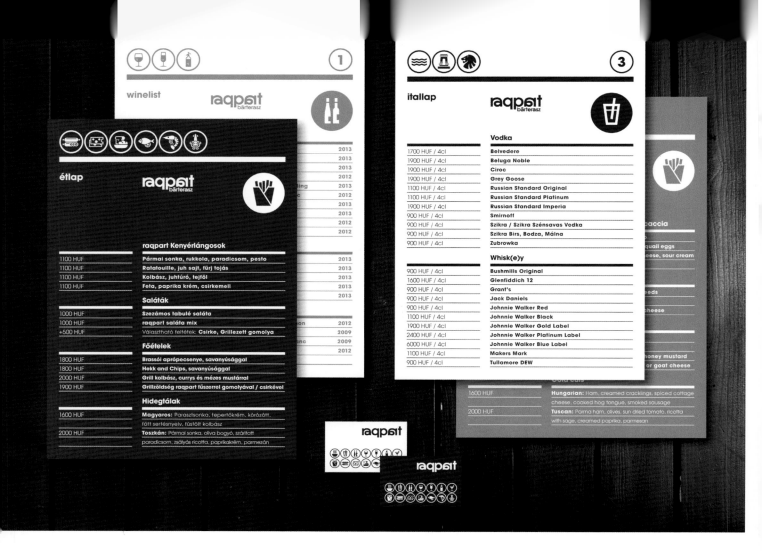

Raqpart

Graphic Designer / kissmiklos
Art director / kissmiklos
Photographer / Krisztián Bódis, Bertalan Soós & kissmiklos

📍 Jane Haining rkp., 1052, Budapest, Hungary

📞 +36 30 464 0646

🍴 Mon – Thu: 12:00 – 01:00;
Fri – Sat: 12:00 – 03:00;
Sun: 12:00 – 01:00

▶ Since 2014

Raqpart is an open–air bar with a relaxing atmosphere in Budapest, on the coast of the Danube. Its location at the bottom of the Chain Bridge provides the perfect view of the Buda Castle. The enchanting relaxed feeling nearby the dock thereupon result in the new branding – blue and white – to engage the guest in the cozy atmosphere. The branding is mainly based on logotype, simple icons, and illustrations that imply the location and the restaurant's menu.

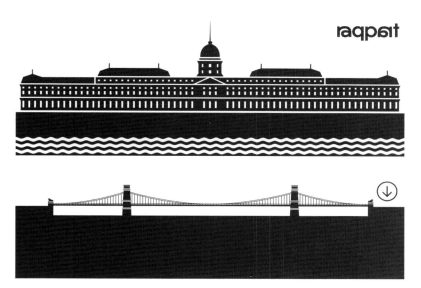

Whisky
Jack Daniels
Johnnie Walker Red
Johnnie Walker Black
Glenfiddich 12

Rum
Bacardi Superior, Black, Oakheart
Bacardi 8

Tequila
José Cuervo Especial Silver, Gold
Patron Silver
Patron XO Café

900 HUF / 4cl
1100 HUF / 4cl
1700 HUF / 4cl
1900 HUF / 4cl

900 HUF / 4cl
1100 HUF / 4cl

700 HUF / 4dl
700 HUF / 4dl
600 HUF / 4dl

Vodka
Szikra/ Szikra szénsavas vodka
Russian Standard Original
Belvedere
Grey Goose

Gin
Gordons
Hendricks

Sör
Heineken
Edelweiss
Soproni

Hay Market

Design Agency / Foreign Policy Design Group   **Creative Director** / Yah–Leng Yu
Art Director / Yah–Leng Yu   **Designer** / Liquan Liew, Vanessa Lim & Yah–Leng Yu

📍 2/F, Grandstand II, Sha Tin Racecourse, Sha Tin, Hong Kong, China

📞 +65 6438 0400

🍽 Match Day: 11:30 – 18:00; 18:15 – 23:00

▶ Since January, 2014

Hay Market is a restaurant located in the sprawling grounds of the Hong Kong Jockey Club. With Hong Kong Jockey Club's pedigree as a British Colonial entity, the basis of the brand personality and language is British Eccentricity. The brand's logo is a playful update on classic letterforms and also functions as a blank canvas, allowing for quirky permutations when combined with different illustrations.

Inspired by vibrant jockey silks which are drenched in centuries of tradition and superstition, the restaurant's visual language is an eclectic mix of bold geometric shapes juxtaposed against vintage British typography and Victorian illustrations from old advertisements.

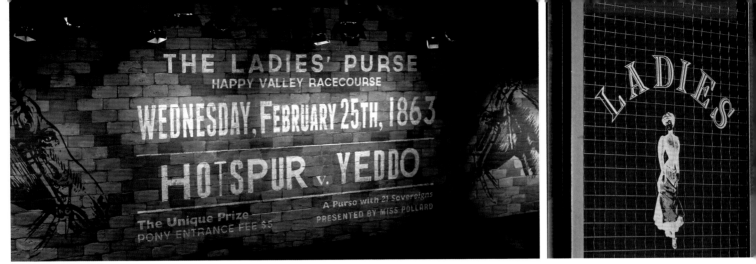

Blacktail Florist

📍 332 Water St #200, Vancouver,
BC V6B 1B6, Canada

📞 +1 604-699-0249

🍴 Sun – Thu: 16:00 – 23:00;
Fri & Sat: 16:00 – 02:00

▶ Since 2014

Design Agency /
Glasfurd & Walker (Branding)
& Ste Marie (Interior)
Creative Director /
Phoebe Glasfurd (Branding)
& Craig Stanghetta (Interior)

Tucked among Gastown's trademark brick buildings, Blacktail Florist
shines a spotlight on some of British Columbia's overlooked and most
humble ingredients. Wild edibles are the inspiration behind daily dishes,
while a range of thoughtfully selected wines by the glass and bottle
showcase the best varietals from this region. The interior design is clean
and bright woodland–inspired. Glasfurd & Walker played off the minimal
interior with a delicate and deliberately feminine style for the design of
menus, photography and custom artwork for the back bar.

Join us for a first glimpse of

blacktail florist

Let chef Jimmy Stewart guide you on a journey through
the edible wilderness of British Columbia. Be one of the
first to experience the thoughtfully composed offerings
in a beautiful space designed by Craig Stanghetta of Ste
Marie Art + Design. Share in the unveiling of Gastown's
newest arrival, Blacktail Florist.

Thursday twenty-seventh of March
Cocktails five-thirty, dinner to commence at six o'clock
200 — 332 Water Street, Vancouver

Kindly RSVP to Michelle Palikot
michelle@hethpr.com

Burger Circus

Design Agency / Substance Ltd
Client / Black Sheep Restaurants
Photographer / Dennis Lo

📍 G/F, 22 Hollywood Road, Central, Hong Kong, China

📞 +852 2878 7787

🍴 Sun – Wed: 11:00 – 23:00; Thu – Sat: 11:00 – 03:00

🏁 Since 2014

Burger Circus is a whimsical take on the classic Mid–century American diner. The space, inspired by Edward Hopper's painting "Compartment C, Car 293," encompasses train carriage accents like the curved stainless steel wall panels and warm tones casted by vintage lamps. The circus narrative in the branding content was derived from Francis Lawrence's Water for Elephants and is pushed throughout the menus and circus posters, which vividly display the different characters' quirks and talents. Situated at the foot of Soho, customers take a ride (almost literally, as they dine in carriage booths) to a nostalgic time filled with retro vibes and feel good food.

Revolver

📍 325 Cambie St, Vancouver,
BC V6B 1H7, Canada

📞 +1 604-558-4444

🍴 Mon – Fri: 07:30 – 18:00;
Sat: 09:00 – 18:00;
Closed on Sunday

▶ Since 2011

Design Agency /
Post Projects (Graphic)
& Ste Marie (Interior)
Graphic Designer /
Alex Nelson & Beau House
Photographer /
Grady Mitchell & Lucas Finlay

Revolver Coffee is a café located in Vancouver BC in Gastown.
Revolver serves up espresso and made to order brewed coffee.
Archive is an extension of Revolver, both in brand and physical space.
Archive focuses on retailing coffee related products as well as serving
as additional seating for Revolver. The two are connected by a glass
door between the spaces.

Archive

A

BY REVOLVER

Revolver

R

BREW BAR · 325 CAMBIE STREET

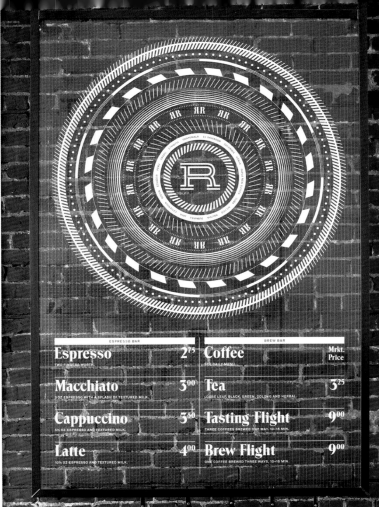

ESPRESSO BAR		BREW BAR	
Espresso TWO FINGERS WORTH.	2⁷⁵	**Coffee** SEE DAILY MENU.	Mrkt. Price
Macchiato 3 OZ ESPRESSO WITH A SPLASH OF TEXTURED MILK.	3⁰⁰	**Tea** LOOSE LEAF, BLACK, GREEN, OOLONG AND HERBAL.	3²⁵
Cappuccino 5½ OZ ESPRESSO AND TEXTURED MILK.	3⁵⁰	**Tasting Flight** THREE COFFEES BREWED ONE WAY. 10-15 MIN.	9⁰⁰
Latte 10½ OZ ESPRESSO AND TEXTURED MILK.	4⁰⁰	**Brew Flight** ONE COFFEE BREWED THREE WAYS. 10-15 MIN.	9⁰⁰

Revolver
325 Cambie Street
revolvercoffee.ca
sheriff@revolvercoffee.ca
604.558.4444

Bowery Lane

Shop 1, Level 4, 1 O'Connell St,
Sydney NSW 2000, Australia

+61 2 9252 8017

Mon – Wed: 07:00 – 22:00;
Thu – Fri: 07:00 – 23:00;
Sat: 17:30 – 23:00;
Closed on Sunday

Since July, 2014

Design Agency / The Distillery
Creative Director / Daryl Prondoso
Art Director / Ben Toupein
Designer / Phil Smith
Construction & Fitout / Calida
Architect / Gensler

By combining rustic charm with shared, farm fresh food, and delicious cocktails, the concept of the Bowery Lane was born. The visual identity was expanded by creating a family of illustrations in a style that evoked The Bowery's farm history. The Distillery employs a sketchy style of illustration, influenced by etching techniques in early news prints. A complete style guide is created to utilize an adaptable, modular grid system, combining the illustrations with sleek and modern typography. To bring the design to life, the designers hand–painted a series of feature murals during construction, crafted a full suite of letterpress printed stationery, menu boards, produced specialty packaging, as well as a responsive website.

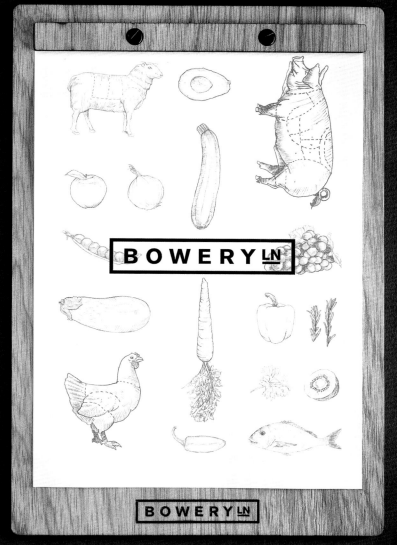

4ECK Restaurant and Bar

Designer / kissmiklos
Photographer / Bálint Jaksa

📍 Johannesgasse 16, 1010 Wien, Austria

📞 +43 1 9744788

🍴 Mon – Thu: 17:00 – 24:00;
Fri – Sat: 17:30 – 24:00;
Closed on Sunday

▶ Since 2015

4ECK breaths a new breeze in the hospitality industry with its brand new direction based on the idea of diversified cultures. Every course was inspired by a city, such as Vancouver – with Canadian salmon, or another one called Budapest – with a traditional egg bread, liver paste and -g marmalade. The dishes set the customers on a culinary journey around the world.

The interior is based on the same concept as well by presenting miniature taxis from lots of cities and can with the names and feelings of different cities. 4ECK is not only for those who like to travel and like to try new food everywhere, but for those who like to be nostalgic and re–live a long forgotten experience. All circumstances are present to have a pleasant time there, among good friends.

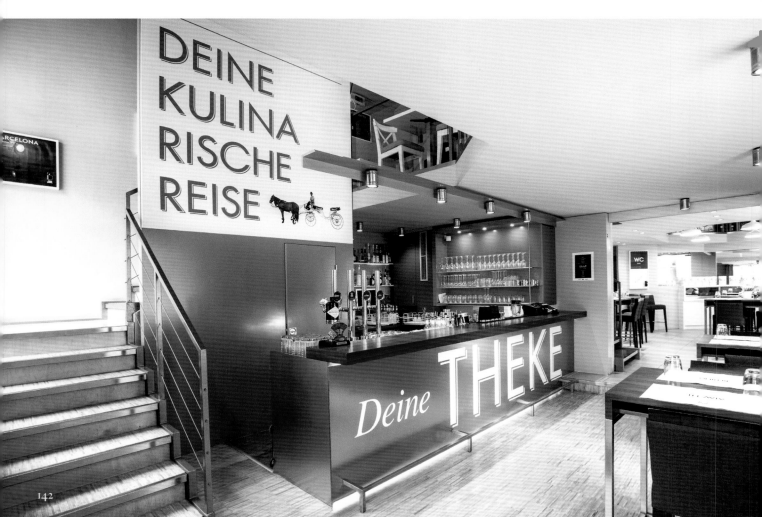

Aguafuerte

Design Agency /
Estudio Yeyé
Designer /
Orlando Portillo & Daniel Escorcia
Interior Design Agency /
Estudio Yeyé & Labor Studio
Guest Artist /
Gerardo Vargas & Francisco Leon

📍 Victoria 823, Zona Centro,
31000 Chihuahua, Mexico

📞 +52 614 413 2130

🍴 Sun – Mon: 13:00 – 00:45;
Thu – Sat: 13:00 – 01:45

🏳 Since 2013

Estudio Yeyé developed the corporate identity, interior design, branding, and editorial design upon three key concepts: beauty, originality and honesty. They seek to represent the essence of the rural Mexican drunk – one that is drowning in this agua fuerte bottle. Also, as a historical site, the place had a great weight of being a cultural icon of the city. The team decided to save all the graphic sense of the time and they dipped into original resources to achieve real texture and achieve a fully Chihuahuan product.

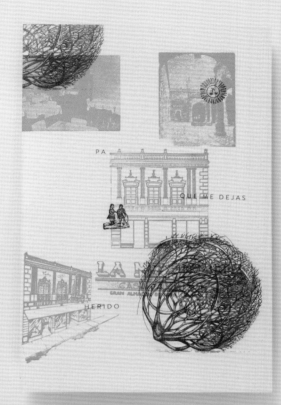

EL AGUAFUERTE CANTINA BRAVA. 100%
VICTORIA **823** CENTRO
NO
DESDE 2013
CHIHUAHUENSE

EL AGUAFUERTE CANTINA BRAVA
CHIHUAHUA CAPITAL CENTRO HISTÓRICO

EL HOMBRE DEL EXITO...

EDUARDO TALAMAS ROHANA
Propietario
12-84-91, 12-84-92 y 12-84-93
REG. ESTATAL 3477

JOSE TALAMAS COMANDARY
Gerente
Gerencia 12-81-67 REG. FED. TARE-641106
REG. CAMARA 117

El
AGUAFUERTE
CANTINA BRAVA
VICTORIA No. **823** CENTRO
chih mex

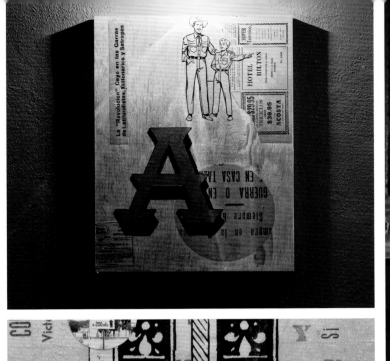

Russ & Daughters Cafe

Graphic Designer / Kelli Anderson   **Façade Designer** / Kelli Anderson
Fabrication / Kelli Anderson   **Copywriter** / Jen Snow
Interior Designer / Kelli Anderson & American Construction League

📍 127 Orchard Street (Delancey Street),
Lower East Side, New York, The USA

📞 (212) 475–4881

🍴 Mon – Fri: 10:00 – 22:00
Sat – Sun: 08:00 – 22:00

▶ Since 2014

Honoring the traditions and history of 100 years of Russ & Daughters, the graphic design was inspired by the original shop's authentic mis–match of typography which had accumulated over the decades—and which gives the space a lively rhythm and human feel. Like the store shelves, the type slotted together like a puzzle on the menu, drink booklets, signage, and bags. The approach is very practical, direct, and durable, but also contributes to the overall impression of being an adult kid–in–a–candy–shop. The layout of the menu reinforces the freeform style of dining experience wherein "sandwiches" are artfully deconstructed arrangements of ingredients on boards.

BY MAMVA
FRESHLY MADE
BY MAMVA
SIP &
MUNCH
OPEN NOW
PLEASE COME IN

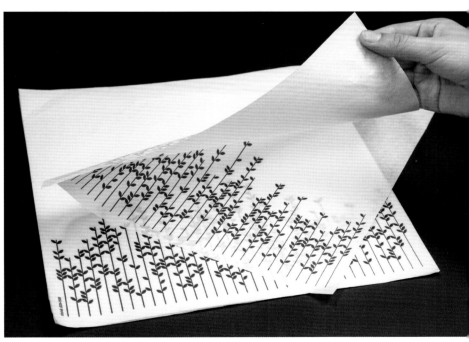

FRESHLY MADE
BY MAMVA

SIP &
MUNCH

OPEN NOW
PLEASE COME IN

Sushi & Co

Creative Agency / Bond Creative Agency
Designer / Toni Hurme
Producer / Piia Suhonen

⦿ On Silja Symphony from Stockholm to Helsinki

🍴 According to each shipment

▶ Since 2014

Sushi & Co. is a sushi restaurant on a Baltic Sea cruise ship that was in the need of a new visual identity. Bond designed a simple and clever logo along with a brand identity. The new design incorporates Scandinavian elements with a sophisticated color scheme and oceanic symbols.

MET

Design Agency / VBN

⊙ The 1979 New Culture Zone, Qiaoxiang East Road, Futian District, Shenzhen, China

☎ 0755-23480815

🍴 Open daily 11:00 – 23:00

▶ Since 2015

Located at the lakeside of Xiangmihu, MET allows guests to enjoy delicious food leisurely at any time. Theme on making friends through food, MET provides homey interior design, food and beverage, and amiable service, encouraging guests to taste food, share joys, and enjoy the hours with family and friends. The simple illustrations represent the happy hour of different people, and deliver cozy life style within a community.

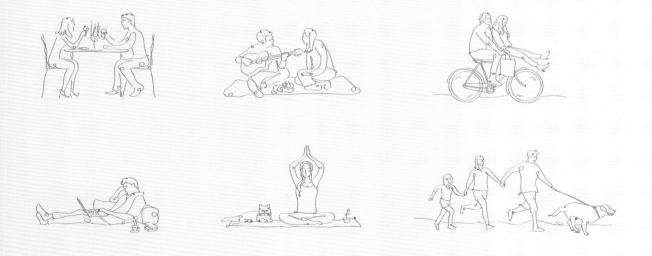

Violet Oon Singapore

Design Agency / BLACK
Creative Director / Jackson Tan
Designer / Lee Xinying
Interior Design Agency / Laank
Photographer / Studio W & Edwin Tan Lumina

📍 881 Bukit Timah Rd, Singapore 279893

📞 +65 6468 5430

🍴 Tue-Fri: 12:00 – 14:30, 18:00 – 22:30;
Sat & Sun: 11:00 – 14:30, 18:00 – 22:30;
Closed on Monday

▶ Since 2015

Violet Oon Singapore is a showcase of Singapore's treasure trove of secret home recipes from their Peranakan heritage while at the same time reflecting Singapore's history as the crossroads of the world with their repertoire of foods from many lands.

The brand revamp reflects Violet's rich heritage background as a Singapore Nyonya and her food journey thus far. The monogram logomark is inspired from the elements of the Peranakan tiles & how Violet used to sign off her articles written at The Food Paper.

VioletOon
SINGAPORE

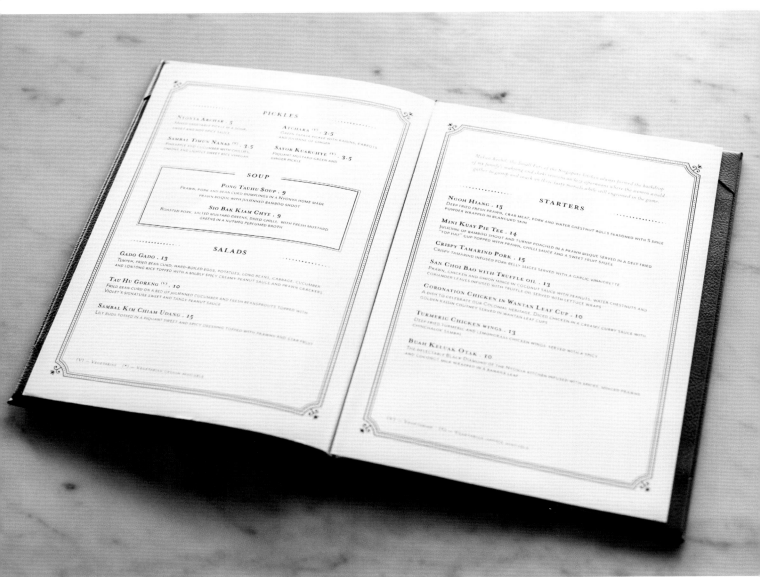

PICKLES

NYONYA ACHAR . 5
Mixed vegetable pickle in a sour, sweet and hot spicy sauce

SAMBAL TIMUN NANAS (V) . 3.5
Pineapple and cucumber with chillies, onions and lightly sweet rice vinegar

ATCHARA (V) . 3.5
Green papaya pickle with raisins, carrots and julienne of ginger

SAYOR KUAKCHYE (V) . 3.5
Piquant mustard green and ginger pickle

SOUP

PONG TAUHU SOUP . 9
Prawn, pork and bean curd dumplings in a Nyonya home made prawn bisque with julienned bamboo shoot

SIO BAK KIAM CHYE . 9
Roasted pork, salted mustard greens, dried chilli, with fresh mustard greens in a nutmeg perfumed broth

SALADS

GADO GADO . 13
Tempeh, fried bean curd, hard-boiled eggs, potatoes, long beans, cabbage, cucumber and lontong rice topped with a mildly spicy creamy peanut sauce and prawn crackers

TAU HU GORENG (V) . 10
Fried bean curd on a bed of julienned cucumber and fresh beansprouts topped with Violet's signature sweet and tangy peanut sauce

SAMBAL KIM CHIAM UDANG . 15
Lily buds tossed in a piquant sweet and spicy dressing topped with prawns and star fruit

Makan kechil, the Small Eats of the Singapore kitchen always formed the backdrop of my family's makning and cheki sessions on late afternoons where the women would gather to gossip and snack on these tasty morsels while still engrossed in the game.

STARTERS

NGOH HIANG . 15
Deep fried fresh prawn, crab meat, pork and water chestnut rolls seasoned with 5 spice powder wrapped in beancurd skin

MINI KUAY PIE TEE . 14
Julienne of bamboo shoot and turnip poached in a prawn bisque served in a deep fried "top hat" cup topped with prawn, chilli sauce and a sweet fruit sauce

CRISPY TAMARIND PORK . 15
Crispy tamarind infused pork belly slices served with a garlic vinaigrette

SAN CHOI BAO WITH TRUFFLE OIL . 13
Prawn, chicken and onion mince in coconut sauce with peanuts, water chestnuts and coriander leaves infused with truffle oil, served with lettuce wraps

CORONATION CHICKEN IN WANTAN LEAF CUP . 10
A dish to celebrate our colonial heritage. Diced chicken in a creamy curry sauce with golden raisin chutney served in wantan leaf cups

TURMERIC CHICKEN WINGS . 13
Deep fried turmeric and lemongrass chicken wings, served with a spicy chinchalok sambal

BUAH KELUAK OTAK . 10
The delectable black diamond of the Nyonya kitchen infused with spices, minced prawns and coconut milk wrapped in a banana leaf

(V) - Vegetarian (v) - Vegetarian Option Available

Bovino Steakhouse

📍 Rua Formosa, Quinta do
Lago 8135, Portugal

📞 +(351) 289007863

🍴 Open daily 19:00 – 22:00

🚩 Since 2015

Design Agency / Triplesky
Director / Bruno Fonseca
Designer / Tonny Schmidt

Bovino combines striking décor with prime beef cooked
to perfection to produce a unique steakhouse experience.
The inspiration used to create the Bovino logo came from
the act of marking livestock with re-heated irons to identify
ownership in ancient times. Taking this historic reference as
a creative insight, Triplesky designed a new font, which is an
evocative of the branding iron's traditional designs, but gave it
a more contemporary and elegant air. Portuguese cork was the
material chosen for the menus for its natural feel, adding to the
overall aesthetic of this extraordinary venue.

Le Saint Cochon

Illustrator & Designer / Marie-Lise Leclerc

⊙ 11 rue Laurencin, 69002 Lyon, France

☏ +33 4 78 37 18 47

🍴 Mon – Sat: 11:00 – 15:00, 19:00 – 01:00
Closed on Sunday

▶ Since 2013

Le Saint Cochon is a French restaurant in Quebec City. Every week, a pig is prepared from head to tail into fine craft charcuteries. The identity is indicative of the personality of the restaurant: savory, refined, and friendly. The handcrafted illustrations are the artisanal touch that well represents Le Saint Cochon. It is a student project by the designer. The stationery, illustrations, menus, and packagings are all handcrafted.

LES
CHARCU
TERIES

Charcuterie artisanale
Un cochon par semaine...
de la tête au pied.

TERRINE ET PÂTÉ
4 $/100g

Pâté de campagne, pâté en croûte, pâté breton,
pâté de foie, pâté grand-mère forestier,
jambon persillé, tête fromagée en galantine,
rillettes, creton, tête fromagée

SAUCISSON CUIT
4$/100g

Bavarois, à l'ail, fumé

CHARCUTERIE SÈCHE
9$/100g

Saucisson fenouil, romarin, piment, nature,
longe séchée, épaule séchée

CHARCUTERIE CUITE
4,00$/100g

Jambon, tasso (épaule fumée), longe fumée,
bacon de flanc, pastrami, rôti de boeuf,
viande fumée

SAUCISSE FRAÎCHE
3,50$/100g

Toulouse, italienne (vin rouge et fenouil),
poivron rôti, champignons, fromage, raisin
et cidre de glace, boudin noir

Misegreta

📍 Avenida de Las Rosas 464, Local A, Chapalita,
44500 Guadalajara, Jal., Mexico

📞 +52 33 3121 6418

🍴 Mon – Sat: 10:00 – 22:00;
Sun: 12:00 – 20:30;
Closed on Tuesday

▶ Since 2014

Design Agency / Para Todo Hay Fans ®
Design Director / Guillermo Castellanos
Art Director / Moisés Guillén
Designer / Moisés Guillén
Interior Designer / Andrea Caporasso & Francesca Dell' Abate

Misegreta is an establishment dedicated to offering 100% Italian gelato, desserts, confectionery and specialty coffee.
Misegreta is a combination of Italian "miscela" and "segreto," which in English is "secret mix." The logo is consisted
of the brand name and a key, which is the secret of Misegreta's products – passion, love, and Italian traditions.

SỐ. 9

SO 9

📍 CASBA, 1/18 Dank Street, Waterloo NSW 2017, Australia

📞 +61 2 8542 7137

🍴 Tue – Sun: 09:00 – 22:30; Closed on Monday

🚩 Since 2015

Design Agency / BrandWorks
Creative Director / Fiona Gillmore
Designer / Fiona Gillmore
& Jyotsana Gill
Illustrator / Beth Emily

SO 9, which translates to Number 9, is the lucky number in Vietnamese culture. Situated in Waterloo, Sydney, SO 9 restaurant serves up authentic Vietnamese street food in a refined, minimal, and contemporary setting. The brief was to design a brand and store that was an homage to the client's own Vietnamese roots as well as their Australian upbringing. The restaurant melds together traditional street food cues with a pared back interior inspired by the client's love of fashion and Scandinavian design.

BrandWorks invited illustrator Beth-Emily to create several pieces of art for both the interiors and the menu. The quiet, spacious, and reflective style speaks to the concept of families, journeys and collective memory in the illustrations are highlighted as much as in the carefully crafted type which features custom built diacritic accents.

THE GRAIN STORE

Design Agency / BrandWorks
Creative Director / Michael Tan
Designer / Nani Puspasari

📍 517 Flinders Ln, Melbourne VIC 3000, Australia

📞 +61 3 9972 6993

🍽 Mon – Fri: 07:00 – 16:00; Sat & Sun: 08:00 – 16:00

🚩 Since 2013

BrandWorks was engaged in developing a new food concept to breathe life into an unloved area, on the west-end of Flinders Lane. They presented feasibility studies to the landlord to ensure the concept would work, and tapped into the area's rich history of grain and stock warehousing to craft the brand.

The interiors were a collaborative effort between BrandWorks and Betty & Wolff, with each detailed handpicked and sourced from around the world to articulate The Grain Store's heritage. Adorned on the walls, menus and seating are hand painted art works and screen-printed designs, all made by BrandWorks.

Mosquito

📍 32 Water St, Vancouver, BC
V6B 1A4, Canada

📞 +1 604-398-3188

🍴 Wed – Sat: 17:00 – 24:00;
Sun: 17:00 – 23:00;
Closed on Monday & Tuesday

▶ Since 2015

Design Agency /
Glasfurd & Walker (Branding)
& Ste Marie (Interior)
Creative Director /
Phoebe Glasfurd (Branding)
& Craig Stanghetta (Interior)
Interior Designer /
Kate Snyder

Mosquito have a simple offering: a champagne bar without the caviar and a dessert bar without with frosting. Located in Gastown, Vancouver the small room contradicts the expectation of a traditional dessert bar – edgy with a fine balance of masculine and feminine details. The brand created by Glasfurd & Walker draws on the interior design details and adds a layer of sophistication and luxury through custom designed typography, deep color palettes and accents of metallic finishing on printed collateral such as menu's, wallpaper and stationery. The name is an intentional counterpoint to the beauty and nuance of the space – again playing on idea contradiction and expectation.

Madam Sixty Ate

Design Agency / Substance Ltd
Client / Atelia Corporation Limited

◉ 8, The Podium, J.Senses, 60 Johnston Rd, Wan Chai,
Hong Kong, China

☎ +852 2527 2558

🍴 Mon – Fri: 12:00 – 24:00;
Sat & Sun: 11:00 – 24:00

▶ Since 2011

Substance created the exploits of a mythical person that reflected the
chef's vision and the surprise pairing of ingredients. Madam Sixty Ate is a
mysterious adventurer and eclectic writer who delights us with her palate
and imagination. Her world view is modern with a twist, mirroring the
style of food. Her surreal experiences and astounding stories are reflected
consistently throughout the brand using paintings, journal entries within
menus, coasters and ultimately through the cuisine. The journey from
discovering a new restaurant to after dinner farewell is a reflection of the
journey madam has when she discovers the variable species which capture
guests' imaginations.

EVVA

📍 Avenue of the Americas 1528, Guadalajara,
Jalisco 44610, Mexico.

📞 01 33 1562-0609

🍴 Sat – Mon: 21:00 – 5:00; Wed – Sat: 13:00 – 5:00

▶ Since 2015

Creative Director / Roberto Ambriz
Art Director / Roberto De Leon
Designer / Roberto De Leon
Architect / +Arquitectura
Photographer / Antoine Maume

located in the W Hotel in Guadalajara, Jalisco, EVVA blends three different atmosphere into one, club, restaurant, and pool bar. Classical and natural elements were taken for the identity to unify the spaces and applications.

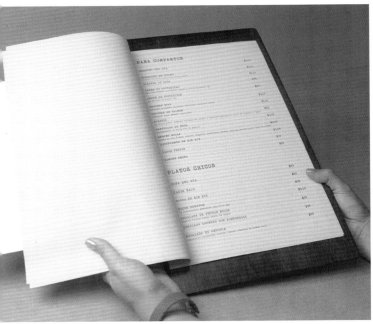

Sal Curioso

Design Agency / Substance Ltd
Client / Elite Grace International Ltd

📍 2/F, 32 Wyndham Street, Central, Hong Kong, China

📞 +852 2537 7555

🍴 Open daily 12:00 – 15:00, 18:00 – 23:00

▶ Since 2012

The Chef of the restaurant has a voice through 'Sal,' and the applications were developed as a form of visual education so they communicate directly with the customer. Substance maintained their mysterious adventurer and eclectic illustration and with a twist to portray Sal's quirky personality, experimental yet technical, which also is indicative of the cuisine. Being an inventor, all the communication materials of Sal are his tools; Therefore, Substance regarded patent applications as menus, annotations are on the wall, labels for devices are business cards and cooking contraptions are displayed as installation pieces.

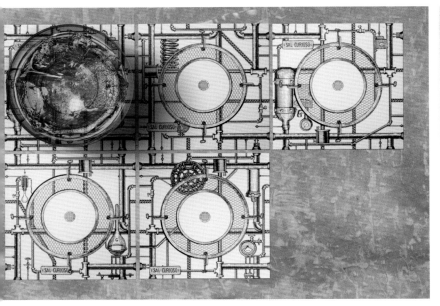

Tamarindo

Design Agency / La Tortilleria

Plaza Mayor, 10, 32005 Ourense, Spain

+34 988 23 87 32

Sun – Thu: 10:00 – 02:00;
Fri & Sat: 10:00 – 03:30

Since October 2014

Located in Ourense, Spain, this restaurant is a typical and refreshing alternative gastronomy spot for local walkers. The architect Ruben Gil D. and his wife Gretta R. Valdés decided to spice up the rainy Galician city with an unusual spot to enjoy international cuisine and drinks in an atmosphere of light wood ceilings, adobe walls, dim lighting, and steel furniture. La Tortilleria worked on the design of its visual identity, stationery materials, takeaway packaging, coasters, menus, and tote bags. A custom made bottle of water on each table welcomes its guests.

Flamingo Restaurant & Bistro

Graphic Designer / Ákos Sarkadi-Tóth
Menu Cover Designer / Rita Koralevics (Paper Up!)
Interior Design Designer / Ildikó Baán (KODU Interior)

📍 Flami Gastro Kft. H-9222
Hegyeshalom Főút, Hungary

▶ Since 2014

The Bistro opens for the younger generation
with its energy and liveliness. Inspired by an
obvious attribute of flamingo bird – as it stands
in the water lifting one foot up in the air – a cut
logotype was made. Letter "L" makes the logo
dynamic as the designers cautiously peek under
the surface for a second.
The designer of KODU INTERIOR developed
a new conception of interior decoration which
resulted in a really bold interior complex.

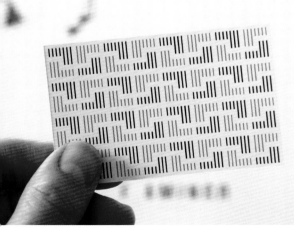

ESPRESSO - tejszínnel **KLEINE BRAUNE**	
	KÁVÉK / KAFFE
HOSSZÚ KÁVÉ - tejszínnel **VERLÄNGERTER BRAUNER**	
CAPPUCCINO - espresso, tej, tejszínhab / espresso / espresso, heisser milch, schlagobers	320.–
MELANGE - espresso, tej, tejhab / espresso, heisser milch, schlagobers	350.–
WIENER MELANGE - kávé, méz, tej, tejhab / espresso, heisser milch, milchschaum milchschaum	420.–
ESPRESSO MACCHIATO - espresso, forlteyi tejhabbal / espresso mit kleine milchshaum	390.–
LATTE MACCHIATO - espresso, sok tej, tejhab / espresso mit kleine milchschaum	420.–
BAILEYS MOKKA - espresso, baileys, tejhab / espresso, mit heisser milch und milchshaum	320.–
IRISCH CAFFE - espresso, whisky, tej, tejszínhab / espresso, baileys und milch und Schlagobers	470.–
CAFFE ALA FLAMINGO - espresso, tojáslikőr, tej, tejszínhab / espresso, whisky, heisser eierlikor, heisser milch und Schlagobers	590.–
ICED LATTE - espresso, sok jeges tej, kávé szirup / espresso, kalte milch und Kaffeegeschmack	750.–
	750.–
	790.–

183

El Passatge

Design Agency / Mucho
Client / Majestic Hotel Group

Photographer / Roc Canals

📍 Rambla de Catalunya, 104, 08008
Barcelona, Spain

📞 +34 935 50 06 06

🍴 Open daily
13:00 – 16:00, 20:00 – 24:00

▶ Since 2012

The logo employs a simple play on the hotel's corporate font, eliminating the serifs between the "l" of "el" and the "p" of Passatge" to accentuate the passage way between the letters as an allegory for the passage where the restaurant is located. Mucho brought in stripes as a graphic element as something very present in marine settings, especially the Mediterranean. There are dozens of objects that recall this graphic motif. In addition, to complement the interior design, nine artists were asked to create nine posters that reflect the character of El Passatge, using stripes as a graphic resource, thus achieving additional variation that complements the graphic language and also brings richness and depth.

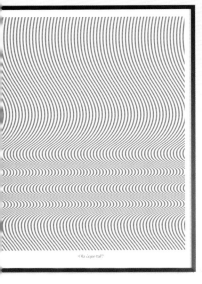

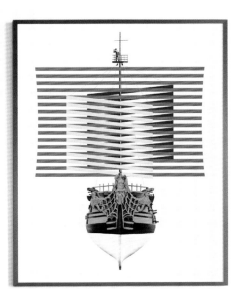

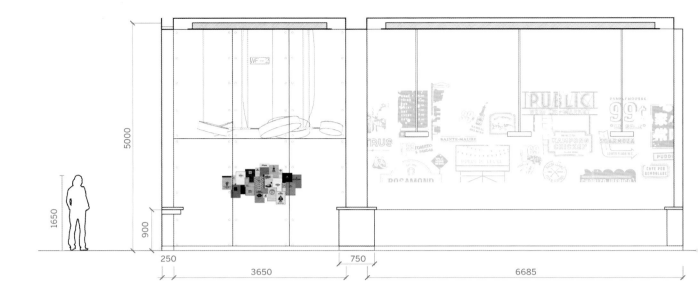

Pidgin

Design Agency / Somewhere Else
Art Director / Madeleine Poh
Interior Design Agency / LAANK

Creative Director / Yong
Designer / Madeleine Poh

📍 7 Dempsey Road | 01-04, 249671, Singapore

📞 +65 6475 0080

🍴 Tue – Thu: 18:00 – 22:30;
Fri: 18:00 – 24:00;
Sat: 11:00 – 24:00

▶ Since 2013

Delightful, curious dishes imagined and inspired by food from the streets, from dreams, from travel and adventure.

Pidgin presents a menu that seeks to surprise and subvert preconceptions. The dishes are a playful blend of traditional Southeast Asian Flavors and inspirations picked up from markets, street vendors or other gastronomic adventures experienced by the Chef.

To express this "hodgepodge of ideas," the identity utilizes a vernacular design language that combines and mixes a variety of different graphic styles. The overall design much like the food at Pidgin portrays an identity that is contemporary with tinges of nostalgia.

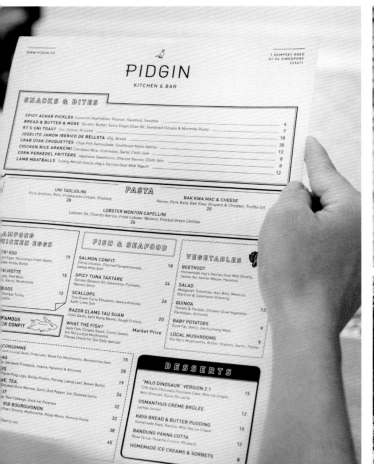

PIDGIN
KITCHEN & BAR

www.PIDGIN.sg

7 DEMPSEY ROAD
01-04 SINGAPORE
249671

SNACKS & BITES

SPICY ACHAR PICKLES Seasonal Vegetables, Peanut, Hazelnut, Sesame 6
BREAD & BUTTER & MORE Border Butter, Extra Virgin Olive Oil, Sundried Tomato & Marmite Pesto 7
RT'S UNI TOAST Uni, Comte, Brioche 18
JOSELITO JAMON IBERICO DE BELLOTA 45g, Bread 38
CRAB OTAK CROQUETTES Chye Poh Remoulade, Southeast Asian Spices 12
CHICKEN RICE ARANCINI Carnaroli Rice, Scarmoza, Garlic Chilli Jam 8
CORN PERKEDEL FRITTERS Japanese Sweetcorn, Chorizo Iberico, Chilli Jam 8
LAMB MEATBALLS Tulang Merah Sauce, Hay's Dairies Goat Milk Yogurt 12

PASTA

UNI TAGLIOLINI
Pork Gratons, Nori, Crustacean Cream, Shallots
28

BAK KWA MAC & CHEESE
Penne, Pork Belly Bak Kwa, Gruyere & Cheddar, Truffle Oil
20

LOBSTER WONTON CAPELLINI
Lobster Oil, Chorizo Iberico, Fried Lobster Wonton, Pickled Green Chillies
26

KAMPONG CHICKEN EGGS

TR* EGG 19
...d Eggs, Hai Loong's Fresh Oyster,
...ster, Konbu Butter

...EURETTE 15
...go, Red Wine,
... Bacon, Mushrooms

EGGS 12
Sambal Tumis,
...ette

FAMOUS
...CK CONFIT

...CONSOMME 15
...with a Local Quail, Prosciutto, Wood Ear Mushrooms, Benedictine Dom

...AS 28
...n, Sarawak Pineapple, Jicama, Hazelnut & Almonds

...S 19
...Farm Frog Legs, Barley Risotto, Parsley, Laksa Leaf, Brown Butter

...NE, TEA,
...moked Bone Marrow, Garlic And Pepper Jus, Roasted Garlic

...IT 32
..., Red Cabbage, Duck Fat Potatoes

...RIB BOURGUIGNON 38
...Pearl Onions, Mushrooms, Kicap Manis, Pomme Puree

...erry Jus 65

FISH & SEAFOOD

SALMON CONFIT 18
Citrus Infusion, Charred Pamplemousse,
Saikyo Miso Aioli

SPICY TUNA TARTARE 24
Sambal Belacan Oil, Calamansi, Furikake,
Wonton Skins

SCALLOPS 26
Thai Green Curry Emulsion, Savory Granola,
Kaffir Lime Salt

RAZOR CLAMS TAU SUAN 20
Clam Dashi, Split Mung Beans, Dough Fritters

WHAT THE FISH? Market Price
Daily Fish, Crispy Sauce, Curry Leaves,
Kin Yan's Local Mushrooms
(Please Check For Our Daily Special)

VEGETABLES

BEETROOT 13
Homemade Hay's Dairies Goat Milk Ricotta,
Jambu Air, Sainte-Maure, Hazelnut

SALAD 13
Malaysian Tomatoes, Ikan Bilis, Mesclun,
Starfruit & Calamansi Dressing

QUINOA 13
Tomato & Pandan, Chinese Olive Vegetable,
Parmesan, Almonds

BABY POTATOES 9
Duck Fat, Garlic, Gochuchang Mayo

LOCAL MUSHROOMS 9
Kin Yan's Mushrooms, Butter, Shallots, Garlic, Thyme

DESSERTS

"MILO DINOSAUR" VERSION 2.1 15
72% Dark Chocolate Flourless Cake, Milo Ice Cream,
Milo Streusel, Dulce De Leche

OSMANTHUS CRÈME BRÛLÉE 12
Lychee Sorbet

KAYA BREAD & BUTTER PUDDING 15
Homemade Kaya, Raisins, Milk Tea Ice Cream

BANDUNG PANNA COTTA 12
Rose Syrup, Sesame Crunch, Rhubarb

HOMEMADE ICE CREAMS & SORBETS

PIDGIN
KITCHEN & BAR

Costa Nueva

San Pedro Garza Garcia,
Nuevo Leon, México

+52 81 8335 4497

StudioDesign Agency / Savvy Studio
Creative Director / Rafael Prieto
Art Director / Eduardo Hernández
Graphic Designer / Ricardo Ornelas

The branding design aims to connect Costa Nueva's identity to Mexico's golden decade characterized by the high aesthetic values derived from the artistic boom the country. "Tan Lejos y Tan Cerca del Mar" (Far Away, Yet so Close From the Sea) is a slogan that emphasizes the characteristic freshness of the ingredients served in the restaurant, as well as the lifestyle evoked by its interior design. The identity is developed a casual and relaxed visual language that reminds guests of a small Mexican beachfront restaurant, and contrasted it with certain contemporary elements, vintage decorative pieces, and a name that explains the concept in a fresh and concise manner.

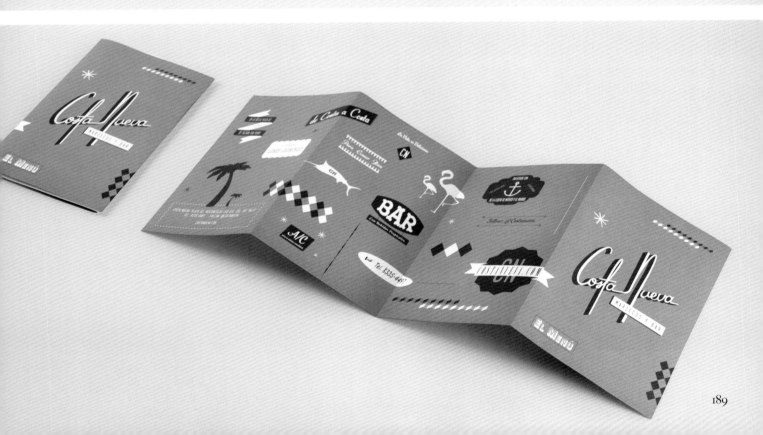

Karhu

Design Agency / Bond Creative Agency
Designer / Tuuka Koivisto, Aleksi Hautamäki, Janne Norokytö, Annika Peltoniemi & Veera Ala-Vähälä
Producer / Mirva Katila

📞 +358 9 444650

🍴 Open daily 16:00 – 02:00

▶ Since February, 2014

Karhu ("Bear") is the bestselling brand of beer in Finland, with a history going back to the 1920's. Bond was asked to give the brand a makeover to ensure its continued relevance in the new millennium. A major part of the project was a branding concept for bars and pubs, which will be implemented into 500 locations around Finland.

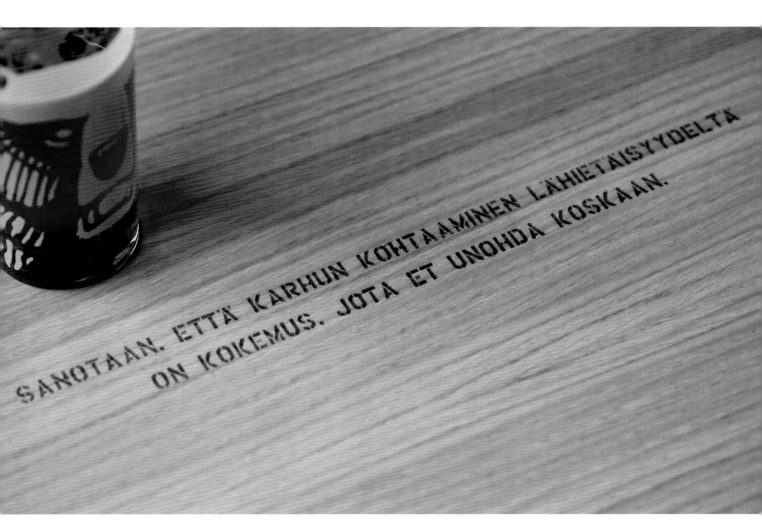

DOB3

Dob Street 3, Budapest
1074, Hungary

+(36)17936783

Since 2013

Art Director / kissmiklos
Designer / kissmiklos
Interior Design Agency / 81Font
(Peter Szendrő & Ádám Bajor)
Photographer / Jaksa Bálint
Client / DOB3 Beer and whisky bar

The objective of the design was to capture beers' essence. kissmiklos aimed to familiarize people with the sophisticated world of beer instead of merely a logo or mark. To achieve this, the final branding was designed to be smart with a friendly, approachable atmosphere.

As the labels of beer vary in many ways, the unique composition was brought up to create a harmony among diverse elements. Moreover, a wall installation made of various beer coasters embarks on a special atmosphere for DOB3.

Snifter

Pint

Tulip

Pilsner

Stein

Weizen

iRISHALE
CREAMALE
imPERIALStOUT
StOUTPOrTER
PAlEALE ale
bElGiAN
FrENCHALE
gErmANALE
WEiSSBiE®
LAMbICFRUiT

MAIBOCK
DOPPELBOCK
MäRZEN
DuNKlERBOCK
gErmANBIE®
lAGERBOCK
SWAR LaGER
ZBiERPIlSNE®
AMERiCAN
iCEBEilLAGER

=== Hello ===

- [ ] EGY FELSŐERJESZTÉSŰ [ ] EGY ALSÓERJESZTÉSŰ
- [ ] A LEGDRÁGÁBB [ ] A LEGOLCSÓBB
- [ ] EGY FINOM AMERIKAIT, AMIT LEGUTÓBB NEW YORKBAN ITTAM
- [ ] EGY ÍZESÍTETT [ ] EGY OLYAN FURA NEVŰ
- [ ] EGY HAZAI [ ] KIVÉTELESEN EGY ALKOHOLMENTES
- [ ] CSAK EGY [ ] ÉN IS UGYANAZT A

| SÖRT kérek. | SÖRT kérem. |

Köszönöm.

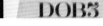

Alberto Senties

Design Agency / Anagrama

📍 Calle Río Guadalquivir 324, Del Valle, 66220 San Pedro Garza García, N.L., Mexico

📞 (81) 8378-6768

🚩 Since 2014

For Alberto Senties, the contemporary, honest and always surprising culinary serving restaurant, Anagrama's design proposal enhances the authoring Sentíes mainly using the seal to communicate their culinary domain. The seal has a typographical game led by the combination of Didot and Akzidenz Grotesk to give an unexpected, modern and elegant touch to the brand. The extensive typographic game that is used by all parts of the brand symbolizes the vast and creative use of textures for the chef in your dishes. His style is clinically clean, precise and true to his town of Monterrey. To demonstrate this, Anagrama put the stain of silver foil on the cards, which represents a portion of the iconic silhouette of the Cerro de la Silla.

The Clifford Pier

Design Agency / Foreign Policy Design Group
Creative Director / Yah-Leng Yu
Art Director / Liquan Liew
Designer / Yah-Leng Yu, Liquan Liew & Adeline Tan
Illustrator / Adeline Tan
Interior Designer / Andre Fu

📍 80 Collyer Quay, Singapore 049326

📞 +65 6597 5266

🍴 Sun – Thu: 12:00-14:30, 18:30-00:00
Fri: 12:00-14:30, 18:30-01:00
Sat: 11:30-14:30, 18:30-01:00

▶ Since April, 2014

Sharing an entity with its heritage, The Clifford Pier draws from its legacy as a bustling port in Singapore during the 1930s. Ginger flower motifs pay homage to William Farquhar who was fascinated with local botany during his time on the island. Collaterals with color palette in sea-foam, coral and caspian blue; classic postage stamps accented with tropical flora and fauna, along with architectural elements, are reminiscent of the glorious voyages that set sail from this historical landmark. Photo courtesy of The Fullerton Bay Hotel.

Lonfood

Design Agency / VBN

No. 34, the 2nd Huancheng Road West, Huicheng district, Huizhou, China

0752-2680200

Open daily 11:00 – 13:30, 17:30 – 22:00

Since 2015

Founded by a group of Chinese designers, Lonfood provides their guests with delicate agricultural atmosphere and aesthetics of life in urban life. VBN was commissioned to design a space that consists of fast food canteen, restaurant, boutique, flower shop, and exhibition hall. Embraced with minimalism, the logo delivers their concept of living naturally and leisurely.

la Florentina

Design Agency / Mucho
Photographer / Roc Canals

 Via Augusta 127, 08006, Barcelona

📞 +34 937 85 11 80

Conceptualized as an everyday restaurant opening 24 hours, La Florentina requested an identity and graphic language to communicate with this business model. A cover of the early versions of Renner's Futura, exaggerating the dot motive of some of the characters to suggest an idea of small ingredients spicing up the structure, is therefore selected and applied on a typographical identity and other graphic collaterals. The composition in the corners, which also provided the idea for the logo, derives from the best line of the brand: "the coffee at the corner." Lastly, the collages mixing old pictures and fresh ingredients link the food with iconic characters.

Hola
encantados
de verte

la florentina

la florentina

Co
mer
cio

Be
per
o

Si el granjero
viera lo que
hemos hecho
con sus verduras,
comería aquí
cada día

la florentina

el café
de la esquina

Tot el que vols des de rush-hour
fins a happy-hour

Obrim tot el dia

12/10

Design Agency / SERIOUS STUDIO

⦿ 7635 Guijo St, San Antonio Village, Makati, 1203 Metro Manila, Philippines

☏ +63 915 663 2823

🍴 Open daily 17:00 – 23:00

▶ Since 2014

12/10 is an izakaya-style dining experience in Makati with an experimental menu. Always pushing to find new territory, 12/10 is a bolder venture for the owners. The challenge was to strike a balance between the bare-bones look and feel of the restaurant's cuisine, and the florid vision of other restaurateurs. The goal was to create a graphical language to deliver a full dining experience. Sleek lines and vivid murals, unique pieces, are carefully placed. The identity and space of 12/10 is a meeting of art and science.

RIB'Z grill&booze

Creative Director / Aleksandar Spasojević
Designer / Milena Savić
Photographer / Senja Vild

📍 Obilićev venac 3, Belgrade, Serbia

📞 +381 11 3286 096

🍴 Sun – Thu: 11:00 – 24:00; Fri – Sat: 11:00 – 01:00

▶ Since 2015

RIB'Z grill&booze is a restaurant offering mostly grilled meat specialties, while it transforms into pre-game cocktail bar at night. It is rooted in their concept that to serve dishes fast and allow guests to enjoy the food leisurely. Designer and architect collaborated to give this venue a disco-butchery vibe. The hand-stamped logo humanizes the brand, and the grid-based menu displays options cleanly. In the interior, bare constructions, concrete and brick walls echoes with the industrial-like and raw atmosphere spiced with authentic hip neon graphics.

GRILL RIB'Z BOOZE

Piće

1 **KAFE I TOPLI NAPICI**

espresso.........................150
macchiato.........................160
espresso sa mlekom.........165
cappucino.........................165
dupli espresso.................170
nes kafa.........................250
čaj.........................190
irish coffee.................250
topla čokolada.................190
plazma šejk.................450
kuvano vino.................230

2 **BEZALKOHOLNA PIĆA**

voda vrnjci 0.25.........155
voda vrnjci gaz. 0.25...155
voda knjaz miloš 0.75...280
voda aqua viva 0.75......280
coca cola.........................195
coca cola zero.................195
schweppes tonic water...195
schweppes bitter lemon..195
fanta.........................195
sprite.........................195
orangina.........................195
limunada.........................195
cedena pomorandža.........195
cedeni grejp.................290
sok nectar jabuka.........290
sok nectar borovnica...195
sok nectar pomorandža..195
sok nectar breskva.........195
sok nectar ananas.........195
sok nectar paradajz.....205
nestea limun.................205
nestea breskva.................210
red bull.........................210
ultra.........................320
golf guarana.................190
190

3 **APERITIVI**

amaro ramma...
mart...

4 **ŽESTOKA PIĆA**

smirnoff vodka.................225
absolut vodka.................225
gin tanqueray.................225
bacardi.........................250
bacardi gold.................225
captain morgan black.....250
havana club 3 y.o.........250
havana club 7 y.o.........430
tequila
jose cuervo silver......235
tequila
jose cuervo gold........235
sambuca molinari........235
absinth angel.................225

5 **RAKIJE**

viljamovka.........................230
kajsija.........................230
šljiva.........................230
dunja.........................230
medovača.........................230
loza.........................230
jezdić šljiva.................230
jezdić kruška.................350
jezdić višnja.................350

6 **VISKI**

johnie walker red.........225
johnie walker black.....345
chivas regal.................345
bushmills.........................245
black bush.................345
jameson.........................245
jameson 12 y.o.........490
jack daniels.................490
four roses.................445

SINGLE MALT
glenlivet.........................245
talisker...
laphroig...

Ananda Vegan Restaurant

Designer / Nebojsa Matkovic
Photographer / Luka Lajst

prizemlje, Petra Drapšina 51, Novi Sad 21000, Serbia

+381 63 1088978

Mon – Sat: 09:00 – 18:00; Closed on Sunday

Since 2015

Ananda Vegan Restaurant is the first vegan restaurant in Novi Sad, Serbi offering a daily menu as well as sandwiches and sweets. Being one of the oldest languages in the world, Ananda means bliss, a state beyond the senses, mind, and spirit. The fusion of past and present was reflected by the stamped and emblem-like logo, revealing a modern beauty of medieval time. The flower pattern in interior on the other hand shows its pursuit of nature. With the sophisticated pattern, Nebojasa aims to depict the rich and considerate service. Ananda restaurant reminds customers to enjoy every bit of food here and now.

Oldhand Coffee

Designer / Magda Sierzputowska
Photographer / Jayme Anne

📍 31962 S Fraser Way, Abbotsford, BC V2T 1V6, Canada
📞 +1 778-779-3111
🍴 Mon – Fri: 07:00 – 17:00 Sat: 09:00 – 17:00 Sun: 09:00 – 15:00
▶ Since 2015

Oldhand is a family owned café based in Abbotsford, Canada. Its owners have years of experience in specialty coffee, hence the name Oldhand, which describes "someone who is very experienced and skilled in a particular area of activity." The name also refers to the term "Old World," as they have Dutch and Norwegian backgrounds. To reflect Oldhand's attention to detail and the fact that everything is prepared with care, a handwriting logo was used. The identity is professional, classic, and meanwhile welcoming, with a reference to Norwegian knitting traditions.

ACCOMPANYING TYPEFACE

Whitney Light

ABCDEFGHIJKLMNOPQRSTUVWXYZ
abcdefghijklmnopqrstuvwxyz
0123456789!"#$%&*/()=?

Whitney Book

ABCDEFGHIJKLMNOPQRSTUVWXYZ
abcdefghijklmnopqrstuvwxyz
0123456789!"#$%&*/()=?

Whitney Medium

ABCDEFGHIJKLMNOPQRSTUVWXYZ
abcdefghijklmnopqrstuvwxyz
0123456789!"#$%&*/()=?

Whitney Semibold

ABCDEFGHIJKLMNOPQRSTUVWXYZ
abcdefghijklmnopqrstuvwxyz
0123456789!"#$%&*/()=?

Whitney Light Italic

ABCDEFGHIJKLMNOPQRSTUVWXYZ
abcdefghijklmnopqrstuvwxyz
0123456789!"#$%&*/()=?

Whitney Book Italic

ABCDEFGHIJKLMNOPQRSTUVWXYZ
abcdefghijklmnopqrstuvwxyz
0123456789!"#$%&*/()=?

Whitney Medium Italic

ABCDEFGHIJKLMNOPQRSTUVWXYZ
abcdefghijklmnopqrstuvwxyz
0123456789!"#$%&*/()=?

Whitney Semibold

ABCDEFGHIJKLMNOPQRSTUVWXYZ
abcdefghijklmnopqrstuvwxyz
0123456789!"#$%&*/()=?

22 Ships

Design Agency / Foreign Policy Design Group
Creative Director / Yah-Leng Yu
Art Director / Yah-Leng Yu
Designer / Willis Kingery

📍 22 Ship Street, Wanchai, Hong Kong, China

📞 +852 2555 0722

🍴 Mon – Sat: 12:00 – 23:00; Sun: 12:00 – 22:00

▶ Since January, 2013

As the sister restaurant of the Jason Atherton-helmed Esquina, 22 Ships inherits and commands the same edge and swagger as inspired by underground tapas joints found in and around Spain.
The brand identity is influenced by its Spanish origins and the location in the Wanchai area of Hong Kong where it was once a pier and a district with abandoned century-old buildings; as informed by its address – 22 Ship Street.

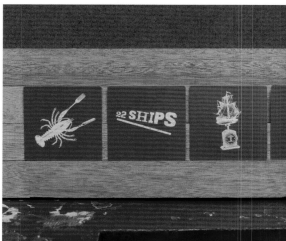

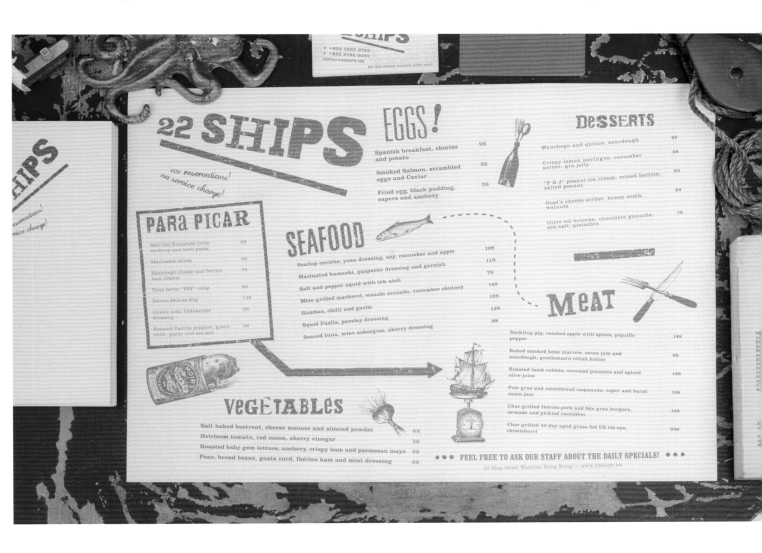

22 SHIPS

no reservations!
no service charge!

PARA PICAR

Salt Cod Brandade Ortiz anchovy and herb paste	68
Marinated olives	48
Manchego cheese and Ibérico ham toastie	78
Tuna tartar "DIY" 100g	88
Ibérico Bellota 60g	128
Oyster with Vietnamese dressing	68
Roasted Padrón peppers, green chilli, garlic and sea salt	68

EGGS!

Spanish breakfast, chorizo and potato	98
Smoked Salmon, scrambled eggs and Caviar	98
Fried egg, black pudding, capers and anchovy	58

SEAFOOD

Scallop ceviche, yuzu dressing, soy, cucumber and apple	108
Marinated hamachi, gazpacho dressing and garnish	118
Salt and pepper squid with ink aioli	78
Miso grilled mackerel, wasabi avocado, cucumber chutney	148
Gambas, chilli and garlic	128
Squid Paella, parsley dressing	128
Seared tuna, miso aubergine, sherry dressing	88

VEGETABLES

Salt baked beetroot, cheese mousse and almond powder	68
Heirloom tomato, red onion, sherry vinegar	58
Roasted baby gem lettuce, anchovy, crispy ham and parmesan mayo	68
Peas, broad beans, goats curd, Ibérico ham and mint dressing	68

DESSERTS

Manchego and quince, sourdough	68
Crispy lemon meringue, cucumber sorbet, gin jelly	68
"P B J" peanut ice cream, mixed berries, salted peanut	68
Goat's cheese sorbet, honey comb, walnuts	68
Olive oil brioche, chocolate ganache, sea-salt, pistachio	78

MEAT

Suckling pig, roasted apple with spices, piquillo pepper	148
Baked smoked bone marrow, onion jam and sourdough, gentleman's relish butter	68
Roasted lamb cutlets, creamed potatoes and spiced olive juice	188
Foie gras and sweetbread empanada, caper and burnt onion jam	148
Char grilled Ibérico pork and foie gras burgers, avocado and pickled cucumber	148
Char grilled 40 day aged grass fed US rib-eye, chimichurri	208

●●● FEEL FREE TO ASK OUR STAFF ABOUT THE DAILY SPECIALS! ●●●

22 Ship Street Wanchai Hong Kong — www.22ships.hk

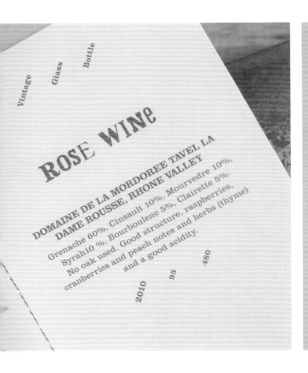

ROSE WINE

DOMAINE DE LA MORDOREE TAVEL LA DAME ROUSSE, RHONE VALLEY

Grenache 60%, Cinsault 10%, Mourvedre 10%, Syrah10 %, Bourboulenc 5%, Clairette 5%. No oak used. Good structure, raspberries, cranberries and peach notes and herbs (thyme) and a good acidity.

Vintage	Glass	Bottle
2010	95	480

Salt baked beetroot,

VEG

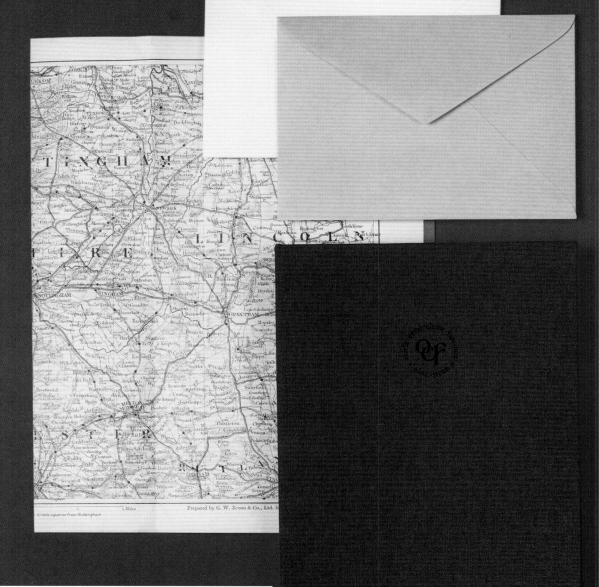

OCF

📍 1 Old Parliament Ln, Singapore 179429

📞 +65 6333 9312

🍴 Mon – Fri: 12:00 – 14:30,
18:00 – 22:30;
Sat: 18:00 – 24:00
Closed on Sunday

▶ Since 2013

Design Agency /
BLACK
Creative Director /
Jackson Tan
Designer / Ng Yong Yi
Interior Design Agency /
Formwerkz

Bringing back the old beauty and charm of the historic rooms in the former Empress Place Building, OCF is a French restaurant reminisces the courtship days of Sir Stamford Raffles and his wife. The branding and menus are kept elegant, mysterious, and personal, like the secret personal love letters.

Mise En Bouche
Petite Pois en "Tiramisu Gourmand", Flavours of Iberian

Scottish Razor Clams, Spanish Chorizo, Sesame Praline,
Essence of Kombu

Roasted Hokkaido Scallops, Gratin of Gillardeau Oysters,
Bouillon with Fragrances of Alsace

Grilled Brittany Seabass, Fricasee of Artichokes,
Aromatic Parsley Jus

Poached Guinea Fowl, Creamed Savoy, Girolles Mushrooms,
Sauce Perigeux

Light Genoise of Muscovado, Mont Blanc Of Roasted Chestnut,
Glace of Salted Caramel

Gourmandise

Mise En Bouche
Petite Pois en "Tiramisu Gourmand", Parmesan Emulsion

Jardinere of Heirlooms Beets, Grains, Sprouts,
Fragrances of Winter

Fine Veloute of Tompinabour, Piedmont Hazelnuts, Girolle Fricasse,
Essence of Truffle

Duo of Asparagus, Poach Organic Egg, Aged Comte,
Sauce of Smoked Courgette

Mille Feuille of Winter Roots, Tuber Melanosporum,
Aromatic Jus of Morels

Gourmandise

168

• CHRISTMAS EVE MENU •

nent Lane #02-02
429
9312
9412
com

were saved except two. We took a little gun-boat
and went for a regular excursion, we made our
round Cape Horn on a lovely fine day, passing
a mile to the South of it. It was quite worth the
as it looked so grand and solitary, rising in
straight up for 1500 feet above the sea. The se
smooth except for the long swell, but that is
to prevent anything good in the way of phot
We looked in at a mission station which has the
southerly church in the world, run by a litt
named Williams... I was bitterly disappointed
the Indians all decently clad & talking
is not what I wanted at all! Then on a
we landed in a lonely bay where we found to
all Austrians, washing for gold, in the sa
beach. Were it not for the beastly cold & the
I would be inclined to settle there with a
a little bucket and return to the innocent
-hood. But the profits were too small, I do
of these men will ever really make anything
it. So many have tried there and failed.
+ then along the south shore of Tierra del ?

A FRANCESIN
QUE SE COME À

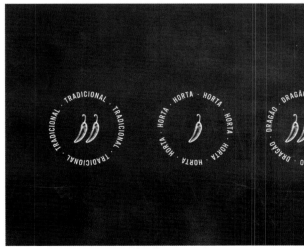

Sandinha

📍 Mercado Do Bom Sucesso,
Porto 4150, Portugal

📞 914216937

🍴 Mon – Sun: 11:00 – 23:00
Fri & Sat: 11:00 – 24:00

▶ Since 2015

Design Agency /
327 Creative Studio
Creative Director /
Mafalda Portal
Art Director /
Mafalda Portal
Designer /
Mafalda Portal & Ana Noversa

327 Creative Studio approached to develop the complete restaurant
experience, involving naming, brand and identity, packaging, website,
social networks, interior design and space planning.
Due to the product's history and tradition, the brand aesthetics and interior
design followed those principles, while communicating in a single color
and with an industrial type and furniture.

Botanero Moritas

Design Agency / Anagrama

66200, Independencia 143, Col. Centro, 66200 San Pedro Garza García, N.L., Mexico

+52 81 8338 8374

Mon – Sat: 13:00 – 1:00
Closed on Sunday

Since 2014

In the project of rebranding Botanero Moritas, its owner, a Mexican ex-boxer, entrusted Anagrama to revamp the place while keeping its rich tradition alive. The objective was to develop a casual environment that placed its regional cuisine as part of the experience. The branding was renovated and modernized alongside the cantina's interiors as well as its kitchen, while maintaining the essence of its past by keeping some of the original décor within the architectonic space. Botanero Moritas creates an environment that allows for a genuine experience typical of a historic regional cantina.

TORTILLAS
RECIÉN HECHAS
No. 20

N° 143

No. 6 FRIJOLES
CON
ASADO

SE SIRVE
CHICHARRÓN
DE PUERCO
de 1 pm a 1 am

No. 3
PAN

No. 9
ARROZ
CON HUEVO ESTRELLADO

DE ELOTE
En caldillo de chipotle

ROJO

MORCON

No. 10
PULPO $105
CON ADOBO DE CHILE MORITA

No. 16
CAMARONES

FLAUTAS

SALSAS

GUACAMOLE

CERVEZA

PAPA ASADA
Y
GRATINADA

BETABEL

SHORT RIB

PUERCO

1939

BOTANERO MORITAS DESDE 1939

No. 143

LECHON HORNEADO Y MARINADO
EN NARANJA Y ACHIOTE

CORTE de
RIB

EYE

FILETE

MOLLEJAS

No. 8

PRIME ANGUS

Tartares & Co

📍 1201, Boulevard James-Fazy 10,
1201 Genève, Switzerland

📞 +41 22 732 09 09

🍴 Mon – Fri: 12:00 – 14:00, 18:00 – 24:00
Sat & Sun: 18:00 – 24:00

▶ Since 2014

Design Agency /
Studio Gambetta
Designer /
Benoît Dumont
& Franco Szymanski
Webmaster /
Jorge Stamatio

Based in Geneva, Tartares & Co is the only restaurant in Switzerland
that specializes in raw cuisine.
The Tartar, being the monument of the gastronomy, is the inspiration
for this design. Resulted from a simple, minimal, and modern
approach, the identity is composed of geometric elements, with
sharp contrast of black and white. The graphic language leads to a
distinguish atmosphere for Tartares & Co.

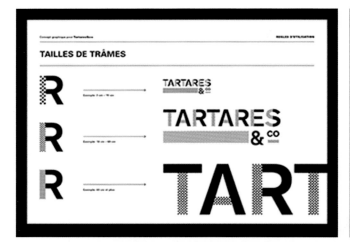

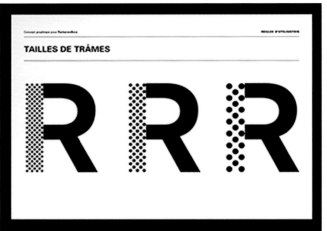

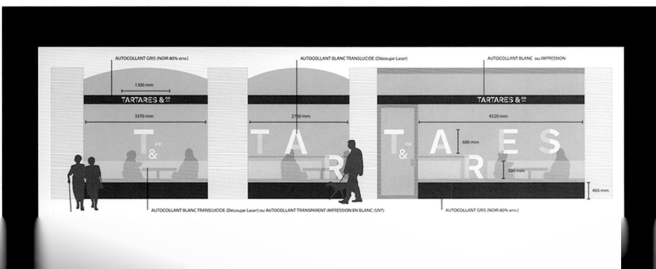

Table Manners

Design Agency / BLACK
Designer / Lin Junyao & Ng Yong Yi

Creative Director / Jackson Tan
Interior Design Agency / Formwerkz

5 Changi Business Park Central 1, Changi City Point — The Oasis #01-68/69, Singapore 486038

+65 6604 7669

Open daily 11:30 – 24:00

Since 2012

A casual restaurant serving comfort food, Table Manners is the least expected place to be called the name. Always staying gracious – but sometimes irreverent – Table Manners promotes proper dining etiquette through engaging and entertaining ways.
From the napkins, to the quirky quotes, and down to the staff uniform, everything comes with a mischievous twist. The acronymic logo mark of the restaurant also secretly hopes to "trademark" everything it can possibly own.

229

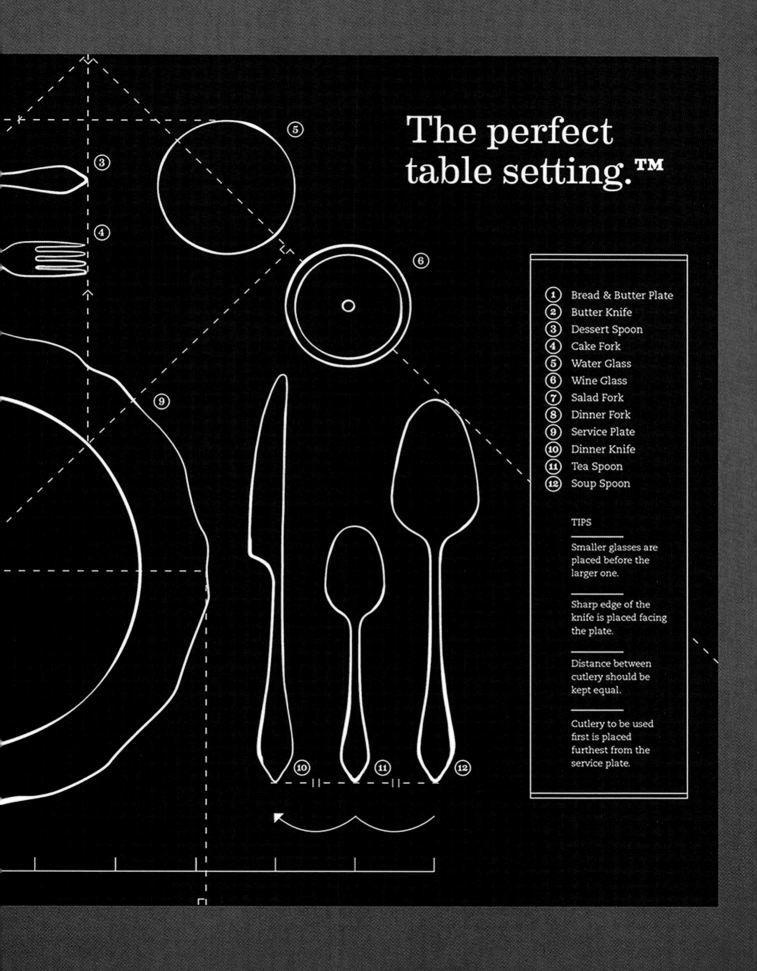

The perfect table setting.™

1. Bread & Butter Plate
2. Butter Knife
3. Dessert Spoon
4. Cake Fork
5. Water Glass
6. Wine Glass
7. Salad Fork
8. Dinner Fork
9. Service Plate
10. Dinner Knife
11. Tea Spoon
12. Soup Spoon

TIPS

Smaller glasses are placed before the larger one.

Sharp edge of the knife is placed facing the plate.

Distance between cutlery should be kept equal.

Cutlery to be used first is placed furthest from the service plate.

INDEX

327 Creative Studio

327 Creative Studio is a small and passionate design studio based in Porto since 2009. They are obsessed with creating beautiful brands on a mission to deliver the boldest creative experiences.
Employing distinctive and global approach in every project, they seek for simple and powerful solutions, with consistent and surprising outputs across all platforms.
In every project, they tailor their thoughts closely with their clients, enabling stronger and unique results based on a clean and structured communication.

www.327.pt

P220 – 221

ADDA Studio

ADDA Studio is a Stuttgart based design agency, specialized in conceptual design, creation and communication. Since 2009, Christian Vögtlin represents it with his holistic principle of creation, centering on the customers' wishes, ideas and views. ADDA's goal is to create an emotional and informative benefit to its clients that is homogeneously aligned with corporate values.

adda-studio.de

P010 – 013; P040 – 043; P108 – 111

Ákos Sarkadi-Tóth

Graduated with a degree in graphic design from Hungarian Academy of Fine Arts, Ákos Sarkadi-Tóth is a graphic designer specializing in logo, identity, and branding.

www.behance.net/akossarkaditoth

P182 – 183

Anagrama

Anagrama is an international branding, architecture, and software development firm with offices in Monterrey and Mexico City. Their clients include companies from various industries all around the world. Besides their history and experience with brand development, they are also experts in the design and development of objects, spaces, software, and multimedia projects. Their services reach the entire branding spectrum, from strategic brand consulting, to logotype, naming, peripherals, and captivating illustration design, architecture and interior design projects, and business based solutions around custom developed software.

www.anagrama.com

P084 – 087; P152 – 155; P198 – 199; P222 – 225

Bienal Comunicación

Bienal Comunicación is a creative studio dedicated to building brands, generating value, and creating links with strategic communication. The studio was founded in 2006 in Mexico with the firm commitment to make functional, built-in, high quality, innovative, passionate, and transcendent work.

www.bienal.mx

P116 - 117

BLACK

Singapore-based creative agency BLACK focuses on developing creative cultures for cities, campaigns and communities through branding, design, and curation.
BLACK was founded with a belief that creativity and culture can make a difference and generate positive social, commercial, artistic, intellectual and emotional value that can enrich daily lives.
BLACK has worked with clients around the globe to create innovative and experimental ways to communicate and engage key audiences worldwide.

blackdesign.com.sg

P160 – 161; P218 – 219; P228 – 231

Blacksheep

Blacksheep is an independent, international and award winning design agency that harnesses the power of creative ideas to help companies and their brands to achieve their objectives. Over the past twelve years they have developed an expert practice within the food and beverage hospitality industry, collaborating with their clients to create iconic and remarkable projects.

www.blacksheep.uk.com

P056 – 057; P072 – 073; P082 – 083; P090 – 093

Bond Creative Agency

Brand-driven creative agency Bond focuses on creating and redesigning brands with a craftsman attitude. Located in Helsinki and Abu Dhabi, Bond serves clients ranging from start-ups to global brands.
The agency helps new business and brands to get started. It also refreshes and revolutionizes existing ones for growth. Bond brings together talents from different fields to create cross-disciplinary solutions within identity, digital, retails, spatial, packaging and product design.

www.bond-agency.com

P156 – 157; P190 – 193

Brandon

Brandon is an award-winning agency based in Ukraine. They help their clients to become better by smart and fulfilling collaboration, and meaningful communication.

brandon.ua

P068 – 071

BrandWorks

BrandWork is a creative studio based in Melbourne, Australia. It lives and breathes in a city best known for its coffee, laneway cafe and food culture and arts. The team is consisted of creatives varying from painters, illustrators, graphic and interior designers, strategists, food bloggers, and café operators. They all share a strong passion – to "redefine the experience", for food and beverage, property, hospitality, and retail. Innovation, co-creation, designing for business growth and success are their evaluation of their projects for their clients.

www.brand-works.com.au

P168 – 169; P170 – 171

Bravo

Bravo is a creative studio making and shaping brands. They develop concepts that embrace bold, artistic, and finesse ideas and styles for their clients.

www.bravo.rocks

P118 – 119

Enserio

Enserio is a Spanish graphic design studio with a focus on simplicity. Being serious but creative, transgressive, and perfectionists, they have a unique perspective and are ambitious to transmit the most with the less.

www.enserio.ws

P058 – 061; P062 – 065

Estudio Yeyé

Mexico creative studio Estudio Yeyé provides graphic design and ilustration destined to various formats, including three-dimensional soltions for interior and objects, and branding and innovative markeing solutions. They target to provide their clients with relevant, innovative work, and high quality works to help grow their business.

http://estudioyeye.com/

P052 – 055; P080 – 081; P106 – 107; P144 – 147

Filip Pomykalo, Marita Bonačić, Negra Nigoević

Filip Pomykalo, Marita Bonačić, Negra Nigoević are part of a Crotian freelance collective based in Zagreb and Dubrovnik. Marita, Negra and Filip are award-winning multi-disciplinary designers, working on branding, editorial design, exhibition design, interior design, and more. Driven by a clean and minimal design aesthetic, their solutions are relevant, balanced, and visually intelligent. They implement critical thinking, extensive research, dialogue, and elaborated process to organize and communicate, or even create content and concepts, instead of repetition or not adopting any specific and strictly defined style and approach.

www.behance.net/filippomykalo
www.behance.net/maritabonacic
www.behance.net/negra

P094 – 097

Foreign Policy Design Group

Foreign Policy Design Group is a team of idea makers and story tellers who help clients and brands realize and evolve their brands with creative and strategic deployment of traditional terrestrial channel & digital media channels. Helmed by Creative Directors Yah-Leng Yu and Arthur Chin, the group works on a good smorgasbord of projects ranging from creative/art direction and design, branding, brand strategy, digital strategy, strategic research and marketing campaign services for luxury fashion and lifestyle brands, fast-moving consumer goods brands, arts and cultural institution as well as think tank consultancies.

foreignpolicydesign.com

P024 – 027; P128 – 131; P200 – 201; P216 – 217

Futura

Futura is an independent design studio founded by Vicky Gonzalez and Ivan Garcia in 2008. Today Futura have expanded and diversified their services based on the requirements of customers and business partners. This boutique seeks to redefine Mexican design values, while preserving the functionality, wit and charisma. Futura specializes in resource optimization, paying attention to every detail. Futura's headquarters are based in Mexico but they have clients all over the world.

http://byfutura.com

P018 – 019

Gemma Warriner

Gemma Warriner is a visual communication designer based in Sydney Australia. Her work reflects her interests in information visualization, food design and brand experience, where she seeks to engage, inform and delight an audience beyond the like-minded. Gemma is the co-founder of Book Eating Press, a boutique publishing company, and continues to design across both print and digital platforms.

www.gemmawarriner.com

P104 – 105

Glasfurd & Walker

Glasfurd & Walker is a boutique, internationally recognized design studio. Established in 2007, the studio specializes in brand creation, development and management across a variety of mediums including print, packaging, online and the built environment.

www.glasfurdandwalker.com

P044 – 045; P074-075; P132 – 133; P172 - 173

Kelli Anderson

Kelli Anderson is a Brooklyn-based multimedia artist, designer, and tinkerer. Her clients included NPR, The New Yorker, Wired, The New York Times, The Brooklyn Philharmonic, The American Museum of Natural History, Airbnb, momofuku, and Munchery.

kellianderson.com

P148 – 151

kissmiklos

kissmiklos, or known as Miklós Kiss, is a designer and visual artist based in Hungary. He is a restless pioneer of the Hungarian design and art scene. Continuously developing celebrated works in fields as varied as fine art, graphic design, and architecture, he believes that good design can improve the world. His lifelong passion is to leap beyond the borders of design and create powerful and stunning works.

www.kissmiklos.com

P028 – 031; P124 – 127; P140 – 143; P194 – 197

Korolos Ibrahim

Korolos Ibrahim is a Sydney based freelance graphic designer specializing in strategic branding, creative direction, and graphic design. As creatives, he has the tendency to see or envision beyond what the average eye can see. His visual but analytical mind aspires to practice all elements and principles of design. He subconsciously eats, breathes, smells, touches, hears and sees design. In all, he believes that it is the implementation of strategy and design in today's marketplace makes creatives unique.

korolos.com

P122 – 123

La Tortilleria

Originally founded in an old tortilla factory building, La Tortillería is a creative company with a passion for images and words with the exceptional ability of turning them into an exquisite reflection of an idea. They create, brand, design, publish and advertise blending creativity and functionality to grant each project a unique personality. They are creative problem solvers who begin with the end in mind either from scratch or from an outlined plan and make things happen come hell or high water.

www.latortilleria.com

P180 – 181

Magda Sierzputowska

Magda Sierzputowska is a freelance graphic designer from Warsaw, Poland. She specializes in creating visual identities for small businesses, but she also enjoys editorial work for magazines. Even though her work is usually clean and minimalistic, it is always well researched and thought through.

www.behance.net/magdasierzputowska

P214 – 215

Marie-Lise Leclerc

Marie-Lise Leclerc is a graphic designer specializing in editorial design, branding, and illustration. Currently based in Quebec City, she is the Art Director and the Print Department's head in Transistor Design Studio.

www.behance.net/marie-lise

P164 – 165

Masaomi Fujita

Masaomi Fujita was born in 1983 in Shizuoka Prefecture. After graduating from the Faculty of Design in Shizuoka University of Art and Culture, he engaged in planning, editing, and directing for several years. He reinvented himself as a designer, and worked in an advertising production company as a Design and Art Director for cosmetics, fashion, and magazines. He established a design office "tegusu" in 2012. Now he performs a wide variety of works from concept planning to design work in CI and VI development for companies and shops, including graphic designs and web designs.

tegusu.com

P120 - 121

Masquespacio

Masquespacio is a creative consultancy established by Ana Milena Hernández Palacios and Christophe Penasse in 2010. Combining their distinctive disciplinary – interior design and marketing – they created an innovative business model that leads to internationally recognized branding projects in design, fashion, and lifestyle trends.

www.masquespacio.com

P020 – 021

Milena Savić & Aleksandar Spasojević

Milena Savić is a graphic designer based in Belgrade, Serbia. Currently she works as a freelancer focusing mainly on branding and editorial design. Driven by simple and clean aesthetics, her works are reinforced with strong and playful concepts.
Aleksandar Spasojević is a New York based architect from Belgrade, Serbia. He founded his own multidisciplinary studio L'enfant Terrible in 2013 with a focus on creative concepts in architecture, design and branding through unique holistic approach.

www.behance.net/milenasavic

lenfantterribledesign.com

P208 – 209

Mucho

Mucho is a global boutique design studio based in Barcelona, Newark, Paris, San Francisco, and New York. Their principals represent multiple cultures yet are dedicated to a singular mission: to define how companies are perceived in the world, so they can stand out and succeed.

They offer creative strategy and design for all kinds of clients — from boutique businesses and start-ups to multinational corporations.
By arranging senior positions at the most renowned design studios and working directly with every client from start to finish, Mucho's tight-knit global office network allows their designers to collaborate across oceans and cultures. This continually infuses their work with fresh perspectives and creates an esteemed pool of resources for every project.

wearemucho.com

P184 – 185; P204 – 205

Nebojsa Matkovic

Nebojsa Matkovic is a graphic designer currently living and working as a freelance designer in Novi Sad, Serbia. After graduating in college of Industrial Management he followed his passion towards illustration and design. After self-taught for merely few months he started his professional career in a design agency based in his hometown Subotica, Serbia.

www.behance.net/NebojsaMatkovic

P210 – 213

Nicklas Haslestad

Born and raised in Norway, Nicklas Haslestad is a designer and art director currently living and working in Oslo. His work process is based on the desire to utilize Scandinavian aesthetics, passion and personal commitment, to create strong conceptual ideas and distinctive, bespoke design solutions.

pocketoslo.com/nicklashaslestad.com

P066 – 067

Para Todo Hay Fans ®

Para Todo Hay Fans ® is a brand media marketing agency based in Guadalajara, Mexico, founded by Federico V. Astorga in 2010. They provide solutions for the creation, diffusion, and promotion for brands. Their services include: web development, multimedia Services, branding, online marketing, social media and advertising. With their work internationally recognized, they worked with clients in worldwide.

paratodohayfans.com

P166 – 167

Parametro Studio

With a broad working scope expanding from concept, digital design, branding, and architecture, Parametro Studio is a multidisciplinary studio delivering new and iconic design.

www.parametrostudio.com/

P022 – 023

Paweł Kozakowski

Paweł Kozakowski is a designer from Poland. He studied graphic design in Academy of Fine arts in ASP w Łodzi. He used to work in several agencies in Warsaw and currently owns his design studio. He is specialized in branding, logo designs, and packaging. Besides, he is fancy for typography, lettering, and sign design.

www.behance.net/pawelkozakowski

P098 – 101

POST

POST is an independent, London-based design agency working collaboratively with clients to achieve clear and intelligent design solutions for identity, print, online and publishing applications.
Led by research and insight, their multi-disciplinary approach allows them to provide a comprehensive range of creative services. They are proud to showcase a wide portfolio of work within many sectors, from fashion labels and art galleries to bars and restaurants. Global or local, they look to build long-term relationships with their clients, growing and evolving their brands over time.

www.deliveredbypost.com

P102 – 103

Post Projects

Post Projects Inc. is a creative services and design consultancy founded in 2011. Post works with local and international clientele on projects that require brand identity, art direction, print, packaging, exhibition and environment design, pattern, type design, and interactive design and development.

www.post-projects.com

P112 – 115; P136 – 137

Roberto De Leon Garcia

Roberto De Leon is a Guadalajara-based art director and graphic designer specialized in branding and advertising.

www.behance.net/robertodeleon

P176 – 177

Savvy Studio

Savvy is a multidisciplinary studio dedicated to developing brand experiences that generate lasting bonds between clients and the public. The team is consisted of specialists in marketing, communication, graphic design, industrial design, creative copywriting, and architecture. Savvy also works closely with international artists and designers, and offers innovative creative solutions with a global competitive vision.

savvy-studio.net

P014 – 017; P046 – 047; P188 – 189

SERIOUS STUDIO

SERIOUS STUDIO is a full-service brand design group dedicated to turning good ideas into great experiences. They are in the business of making brands matter, and building relationships that last. They like working with passionate people who are conscious that design can positively shift the way people think.

www.serious-studio.com

P206 – 207

Snask

Snask is the internationally renowned rockstar creative agency that creates the heart & soul of brands. They create new brands and rejuvenate old ones. They knock off all types of branded material for print, web, film and experimental advertising. Their name means candy, filth and gossip and everywhere they go they make a couple of enemies and millions of fans. After headlining the biggest conferences around the globe they have become one of the most experienced talkers within design and branding.

www.snask.com

P076 – 079

Somewhere Else

Somewhere Else is about the constant shift away from the ordinary; the persistent journey to create work that goes beyond the basal need to communicate. The studio creates distinct and thoughtful work that communicates brand individuality across diverse mediums; transforming brands from mere logos into experiences worth sharing.

www.somewhere-else.info

P186 – 187

Ste Marie

Ste Marie is an internationally engaged, Vancouver-based studio dedicated to realizing inspired and honest design work. They are interested in the intersection of identity, strategy and the human codes that underpin all successful commercial spaces. To that end, their core values are iconoclasm, context and narrative.
They seek to work with likeminded partners and clients to create spaces that are both thoughtful and unique.

stemarieartdesign.com/

P044 – 045; P112 – 115; P132 – 133; P136 – 137; P172 – 173

Studio Eusebio

Studio Eusebio is a graphic design atelier founded in Zurich, Switzerland in 2006. The activities of the studio include all the elements of printed graphic design and digital media. It develops projects with a focus in corporate design, corporate identity, signage, information graphics, editorial design, and web design and interaction design.

www.studioeusebio.com

P032 – 035

Studio Gambetta

Geneva based studio Gambetta was born from the close collaboration between two passionate and qualified designers in visual communication: Benoît Dumont and Franco Szymanski.
This dynamic collective well aligned with its time, offers multiple services within the field of graphic design and visual communication such as art direction, conception and creation of branding, editorial design, poster design, packaging, signage system, illustration, multimedia and web design.

www.studio-gambetta.ch

P226 – 227

STUDIO HEKLA

HEKLA is a global design agency created in 2013. The studio is consisted of four creatives of different disciplines but worked with a common goal.
The diversity of the four designers and their complementarity is a major asset and the global and creative approach. This melting pot offers a transversal and unique look. The wealth and experience related to their different design journey allows them to analyze and understand the different needs of every new client. They conjugate their identity and their skills towards the same target for furniture, architecture or visual identity. The border prosperity of the four creative fields allows them to conceive a coherent project responding to the the client's needs.

www.studiohekla.com

P088 – 089

Substance Ltd

Substance is an award-winning independent branding and design agency made up of obsessive perfectionists, vivid storytellers and a surfboard. The agency was established in Hong Kong by Maxime Dautresme and Florian Michaux in 2011 as a multi-disciplinary agency specializing in brand identity and strategy, advertising, packaging, web and digital design, and interior design. They are curious, adaptable, perfectionists and above all, human.

www.aworkofsubstance.com

P134 – 135; P174 – 175; P178 – 179

Supercake Srl

Supercake is an Italian design studio, based in Milan and Cagliari. It manages different complex projects at various scales, from the preliminary stage to the executive, working with specialized teams.
The design method is intended as a circular process: the sensitivity to the problems and resources (economic, social and environmental), flexibility of thought, originality, analysis and synthesis, intuition and redefinition, carry each project to its aware realization. Since 2014, Supercake became a company that produces and sells its own design products.

www.supercake.it

P036 – 039

The Distillery

The Distillery is a creative studio, specializing in crafting brands, stationery, and cultural events. Heritage soul with modern minds as their concepts, they help position brands with design which is seen, felt, and experienced. As an agency of strategists, artists, and craftsman, they bring them into the world with their hands instead of merely dreaming up big ideas. As creative professionals with a passion for tactility, they believe that the best ideas start and are lived outside a computer screen. They offer branding and design services to a range of commercial clients and individuals. As a production studio, The Distillery is one of the world's leading modern letterpress practices, with a mission to help spread the love of letterpress in Australia, South East Asia, and around the world.

the-distillery.com.au

P138 – 139

Triplesky Branding Agency

Triplesky is a design studio, working in various disciplines, with the ability to lift business to new levels. Triplesky is capable of designing brands in a new dimension and on a planetary scale, fighting the force of gravity to make them all the more valuable and able to soar. They aim to build a team that is visionary, specialized, and multi-disciplinary, which is strongly committed to developing brands from a 360-degree perspective. Each project is lived and breathed in the studio, from start to finish.

www.triplesky.pt

P162 – 163

VBN

VBN established in 2008, focusing on brand creation and design. The core of VBN is "Cross Thinking & Systematic Innovation". VBN improves its elaborative faculties and working modes constantly to attract more foreseeing clients by the initial idea "Crossover, Mix &Match, Graft" to the thoughts of "How to design creatively, how to lead the industry notions."
VBN expands its work by systematical innovations which includes but not limited to concept innovation, strategy innovation, brand planning, graphic design, interior design, web, and multimedia design.

www.vbn.hk

P158 – 159; P202 – 203

Xavi Martinez Robles

Xavi Martinez Robles is a graphic designer based in Barcelona. He is specialized in branding and editorial design but he also works on a broad range of projects like packaging, website, motion graphics, and video.

www.xavimartinez.eu

P048 – 051

ACKNOWLEDGEMENTS

We would like to thank all of the designers involved for granting us permission to publish their works, as well as all of the photographers who have generously allowed us to use their images. We are also very grateful to many other people whose names do not appear in the credits but who made specific contributions and provided support. Without these people, we would not have been able to share these beautiful works with readers around the world. Our editorial team includes editor Javier Zheng and book designer Chen Yingqiao, to whom we are truly grateful.